# Register variation and language standards in Czech

*Neil Bermel*

2000
LINCOM EUROPA

Published by LINCOM EUROPA 2000.


All correspondence concerning *LINCOM Studies in Slavic Linguistics* should be addressed to:


LINCOM EUROPA
Freibadstr. 3
D-81543 Muenchen

LINCOM.EUROPA@t-online.de
http://home.t-online.de/home/LINCOM.EUROPA

*100 2228978*

T

Printed in E.C.

Die Deutsche Bibliothek - CIP Cataloguing-in-Publication-Data

A catalogue record for this publication is available from Die Deutsche Bibliothek (http://www.ddb.de)

Printed on chlorine-free paper

*62242*

*for Celina*
*and*
*in memory of Frank*

# CONTENTS

Acknowledgments ................................................................................................................... 1
0.   About the topic .............................................................................................................. 3
1.   Defining the issues ........................................................................................................ 5
     1.1.  Language medium ................................................................................................. 5
     1.2.  Language register .................................................................................................. 6
     1.3.  Codes and code-switching .................................................................................... 7
     1.4.  Diglossia ................................................................................................................ 9
     1.5.  Conventions and notation .................................................................................... 10
2.   The Czech language situation ...................................................................................... 12
     2.1.  Historical background ......................................................................................... 12
     2.2.  Synchronic background ....................................................................................... 13
     2.3.  How different are Standard and Common Czech? ............................................... 17
     2.4.  Outline of Czech ................................................................................................. 21
3.   The relationship between standard and non-standard forms ....................................... 26
     3.1.  Exclusivity and distinctness of codes ................................................................ 27
     3.2.  Historical factors interfering in descriptive work .............................................. 28
     3.3.  Czech as an example of diglossia ....................................................................... 33
     3.4.  Empirical work on language values and language usage ..................................... 34
     3.5.  Predicting usage from values ............................................................................. 37
     3.6.  The inductive approach to varieties .................................................................... 40
     3.7.  Reevaluating the use of data on language varieties ............................................ 44
     3.8.  Colloquial Czech ................................................................................................ 45
4.   The current study ......................................................................................................... 47
     4.1.  Works in the corpus ............................................................................................ 47
     4.2.  Coding and analysis of the corpus ...................................................................... 48
     4.3.  Authorship and the publication process ............................................................. 49
5.   Analysis by feature type .............................................................................................. 50
     5.1.  Phonemic features .............................................................................................. 50
     5.2.  Morphological features ....................................................................................... 55
     5.3.  Syntactic features ............................................................................................... 61
     5.4.  Lexical features .................................................................................................. 73
6.   Profiles of usage .......................................................................................................... 80
     6.1.  Ivan Klíma ......................................................................................................... 80
     6.2.  Lenka Procházková ............................................................................................ 82
     6.3.  Pavel Kohout ...................................................................................................... 84
7.   Revisiting the SC-CC interface ................................................................................... 90
     7.1.  Validity of phonemic hierarchies ....................................................................... 90
     7.2.  Relevance of morphology-related hierarchies .................................................... 92
     7.3.  Applicability of code-switching models ............................................................. 94
     7.4.  An alternate account of phonological correspondences ...................................... 99
     7.5.  Developing a scale-based model ....................................................................... 103
     7.6.  Final excursus on Colloquial Czech ................................................................. 109
     7.7.  Reinterpreting the four "layers" of the interface .............................................. 110
8.   Conclusions ............................................................................................................... 113

Bibliography ..................................................................................................... 116
Appendix 1. The Czech alphabet and IPA phonemic equivalents ...................... 122
Appendix 2. Glossary of morphology chart abbreviations.................................. 123
Appendix 3. The four major phonological correspondences between SC and CC ............ 124
Appendix 4. Corpus coding tags ........................................................................ 125
Appendix 5. Token counts.................................................................................. 127
Index ................................................................................................................. 131

## CHARTS, MAPS AND FIGURES

1.2.1. Linguistic medium vs. linguistic register................................................. 7
1.5.1. Labels for phonemic variation. .................................................................. 11
2.2.1. Schematic map of the Czech Republic .................................................... 15
2.3.1. Distinguishing features of SC and CC .................................................... 18
2.4.1. Vowel inventory of SC and CC ................................................................ 21
2.4.2. Adjectives ("hard" declension): *dobr-ý* 'good'...................................... 23
2.4.3. Verbs (all major classes) ........................................................................ 24
2.4.4. Nouns (four common declensions) .......................................................... 25
3.0.1. The word 'apple' in four realizations...................................................... 27
3.2.1. Phonemic changes in early modern Czech .............................................. 28
3.2.2. Order of phonemic changes in early modern Czech ................................ 29
3.2.3. Graphemes vs. phonemes......................................................................... 31
3.2.4. Some SC and CC morphological variants................................................ 32
3.4.1. Kučera 1955 ............................................................................................ 35
3.4.2. Kravčišinová and Bednářová 1968 ......................................................... 36
3.5.1. Kučera's possible variants for Adj-N combinations ................................ 37
3.5.2. The instrumental plural adjective ending................................................. 38
3.5.3. Condensation of morphology-phonology hierarchies in Kučera 1973 .... 39
3.6.1. Idealized distribution of functions for *vý-*/*vej-* ................................... 40
3.6.2. Actual distribution of functions .............................................................. 41
3.6.3. Hronek's classifications (1972:19-22) ..................................................... 42
3.6.4. Čermák's grades for CC features (1987:142) .......................................... 42
3.6.5. Bílý's classification revisited .................................................................. 43
5.0.1. Marked tokens in thousand-word samples............................................... 50
5.1.1. CC phonemic variants in SC dialogue, by frequency .............................. 51
5.1.2. CC phonemic variants, by type and frequency ........................................ 52
5.1.3. Tabular format for data from 5.1.2 .......................................................... 53
5.2.1. Source of CC forms................................................................................. 55
5.2.2. CC verbal morphology in dialogue of SC texts ....................................... 57
5.2.3. Tabular form of chart 5.2.2 ..................................................................... 58
5.2.4. Percentage of CC forms in written dialogue and speech ......................... 59
5.3.1. Syntactic features coded........................................................................... 64
5.3.2. Occurrence of features in the corpus........................................................ 65
5.3.3. Sentence length in written texts ............................................................... 66
5.3.4. Simple vs. compound and complex sentences .......................................... 67

5.3.5. Simple and compound vs. complex sentences ............................................................ 68
5.3.6. Features of unplanned speech in each sample. ........................................................ 72
5.4.1. Marking of lexical features in the SSJČ ................................................................. 74
5.4.2. Differences in classification of the lexicon .............................................................. 76
5.4.3. Non-SC tokens ..................................................................................................... 77
5.4.4. Stratification of non-SC tokens ............................................................................. 78
5.4.5. Lexical overlapping: some partial sets ................................................................... 79
6.1.1. Morphology cline in Klíma ................................................................................... 81
6.2.1. Morphology cline in Procházková ......................................................................... 83
6.3.1. Quasi-phonetic spellings in Kohout ...................................................................... 86
6.3.2. Morphology cline in Kohout ................................................................................. 88
3.4.1. (Repeated.) Kučera 1955 ...................................................................................... 91
3.5.2. (Repeated.) The instrumental plural adjective ending ............................................. 92
7.2.1. Kučera's morphology hierarchies in the corpus ..................................................... 93
7.3.1. Communicative code-switching "triggers" (Auer 1995) ......................................... 95
7.4.1. Morphophonemic influence on use of CC /ɛj/, /iː/ .................................................. 99
7.4.2. Long vowels in SC and CC desinences .................................................................. 100
7.4.3. Phonemes reinterpreted as morphemes .................................................................. 101
7.4.4. Common words with initial /(v)o/ .......................................................................... 102
7.5.1. Registers of Czech in literary dialogue .................................................................. 105
7.5.2. Graphic representation of variant competition. ........................................................ 107
7.5.3. Three texts and their register usage ........................................................................ 108

## Acknowledgments

This research was supported by the University of Sheffield International Strategy Group, which underwrote several trips to Prague, and the University's Learned Societies Fund, which supported the dissemination of this research through conference presentations. I am deeply grateful to Professor Petr Sgall of Charles University, Prague, for his detailed comments on early versions of the manuscript, as well as to Professor Karen Gammelgaard of the University of Oslo and Mr. Nigel Gotteri of the University of Sheffield, for graciously taking the time on short notice to read the full version and give many helpful suggestions.

The book was typeset in EuroTimes and IPATimes (from Ecological Linguistics Fonts) on a Macintosh computer using Microsoft Word.

Neil Bermel
University of Sheffield
Sheffield, England
Autumn 1999

1

# 0. About the topic

Academic conclusions about the nature of language varieties should be grounded in objective facts and data. Translating a study of *language variety* into a piece of *language planning* is a different, entirely separate endeavor. As anyone who has looked at the problem in Czech knows, these two fields have traditionally been closely linked. Czech scholars investigating the boundaries and characteristics of language varieties have often applied their conclusions to the debate over the extent to which non-standard features should be incorporated into the standard language, with the polar positions (held by very few these days) being that most features characteristic of the predominant spoken interdialect should officially replace those characteristic of the standard, or that a newly purified standard should be propagated widely, with a view to supplanting the interdialects in some of their traditional spheres of usage.

Language culture in the Czech Republic is a lively and active field, with abundant interaction between the public and academia. Many eminent linguists in the Czech Republic contribute regularly to the popular media and are active in language education policy, and their views on the Czech language rapidly become well-known. In these circumstances, it may be inevitable that much research is read with an eye to its contribution to the language planning debate.

In contributing a study on the standard variety of Czech, I may in a sense be inviting its — and my — inclusion into that debate. However, as a non-native speaker of Czech and an American-trained academic based in the UK, I will not presume to extend the results of this survey to argue for or against developments in language culture: what shall be taught in schools, what shall be permitted or considered "good form" in newspapers and broadcast media, what shall be reflected in dictionaries. While I believe scholarly reevaluation of the status of Czech's varieties is overdue, this account is an examination of a particular descriptive problem in portraying the speech of a particular region of the Czech Republic. It does not assess the desirability of change in the propagation or use of these varieties — whether in Bohemia, in Sheffield, or elsewhere.

# 1. Defining the issues

Czech has attracted attention for its relatively complex and pervasive language stratification. A simplified, "received" view of the language might run as follows: a *standard variety* of the language used primarily in writing is juxtaposed against a widespread *nonstandard variety* primarily used in speech. The existence of a spoken version of the standard and of a commonly accepted method for rendering the predominant nonstandard variety in writing complicate the picture further by giving each variety the appearance of having a more or less complete range of *potential functions*, even if the *actual functions* of these varieties are restricted in a number of ways that will be discussed later. Numerous differences in phonology, morphology, syntax and the lexicon support the view that these two varieties are separate linguistic *codes*, manipulated by users of the language through *code-switching*. In this study I will examine some of the claims inherent in this "received view" and try to situate Czech in a broader context, comparing and contrasting the copious data collected and analyzed by earlier scholars with new data from literary texts. I will show that at certain junctures these data make it difficult to support a view of Czech as consisting of two or more strictly stratified codes that are defined by the presence or absence of code-marking features. In my view, the possibilities for mixing and combining variants of these features is complex enough that we are better off starting from a different picture: one in which different registers combine variants of differing values in various proportions.

## 1.1. Language medium

It is safe to venture that in no language can you write in precisely the way you speak and expect the product to be accepted as more than marginally literate discourse. Conversely, much written discourse seems overly formal or unnatural when read aloud. All languages with an established literary culture develop and maintain different protocols (explicit or otherwise) for writing and speaking, and these divergences are partly a natural consequence of the differences between the written medium and the spoken one.[1]

Pragmatic considerations can explain many of the differences between speech and writing. Unscripted speech is typically conducted in the presence of an interlocutor (in person or remotely); it is not subject to revision or review once formulated; it makes provision for the participation of the interlocutor, as well as for methods of preventing or forestalling his participation where appropriate. Writing is usually conducted out of the presence of the addressee; it is revisable and searchable; it does not need to make provision for the addressee's participation.[2] Research in the field of discourse analysis has outlined the ways in

---

[1] Vachek 1989 discusses many of these issues in a cross-linguistic perspective.

[2] There are natural areas of overlap, such as scripted speech, which need to be considered. In addition, technology has given us interesting hybrid forms that break the pragmatic "conditions" set above, such as "chat rooms" on computer networks and "letters"

which unscripted speech differs from writing (or from written texts read aloud).[3] Some such features are unique to particular languages, but among them are almost always: phonetic differences decreasing the effort involved in pronunciation (truncation, contraction, simplification of consonant clusters); and syntactic differences, such as the predominance of parataxis over hypotaxis, the increased availability and use of deictic forms and words with an appelative function, turn-taking indicators, structures that shift word order in ways not usually found in written language, and so forth. It is safe to regard these features as belonging to *spoken media* vs. *written media*, whether considered as a dichotomy or a continuum.

## 1.2. Language register

Many obvious differences, however, are not as easy to attribute directly to the medium of communication. The nature of the communicative situation can also have an effect on the choice of language produced on any given occasion and situation. The differing varieties of a language in use on these different occasions are termed *registers*.[4] There are a number of ways of demarcating registers. One is by the presence or absence of certain formal features (syntactic constructions, grammatical forms, lexical items), while another is more statistical in nature, checking the frequency of these features.

To take an example of how register differs from medium: English speakers easily recognize the difference between *uncontracted and contracted forms* as one such shibboleth. From an early age we are taught that we may say *don't, won't, can't* but must write *do not, will not, cannot*, etc. Yet this distinction is not purely one of medium. Within written media, consistent use of uncontracted forms is awkward and formal in letters and quotations of spoken English, while it may seem perfectly appropriate in more formal speech. The contracted forms have analogous limitations and extensions. Heated debates occur over the use of contractions in types of writing that are not clearly defined as either formal or informal; for example, writers of instructional manuals are sharply split over whether contractions may or may not be used in their work.[5] There is no way to avoid making a stylistic impression in

---

recorded on tape. (See Čmejrková 1997 for a discussion of the character of e-mail.) The informality and stream-of-consciousness character of some e-mail exchanges has provoked interest among scholars as well. Still, as of this writing, these are peripheral areas, and the basic pragmatic divisions between written and spoken media are still valid for most communicative acts.

[3]  The spoken language unit at the Czech Language Institute, Czech Academy of Sciences has conducted numerous studies of spoken Czech in its various forms; see especially the work of Müllerová, Čmejrková and Hoffmannová, some of which is cited in the bibliography.

[4]  Biber defines a register as "any language variety associated with particular situational or use characteristics" (1994:351).

[5]  Andrew Swartz, Harlequin plc, Manchester UK (personal communication)

the use of contractions: the addresser is choosing a formal mode or an informal mode of presentation, regardless of the medium.[6]

For any language with a long-standing written tradition, we could thus start from a model along the lines of the one in chart 1.2.1.

**Chart 1.2.1. Linguistic medium vs. linguistic register**

| *medium (across)* *register (down)* | *writing* | *speaking* |
|---|---|---|
| *formal, official* | official/formal writing | official/formal speech |
| *informal, unofficial* | unofficial/informal writing | unofficial/informal speech |

This model would, of course, be an oversimplification,[7] but it could serve as a framework for further development. A similar scheme is proposed, for example, by Eckert 1993 (6-7; 9-10) and traces can be seen in the more elaborate register "dimensions" proposed and amply documented for English by Biber (1988).

**1.3. Codes and code-switching**

In some instances the differences between the varieties employed in these situations can be great enough and systematic enough that it is convenient to define them as separate *codes*. The term *code* is preferable here to *language* because it takes in a wider range of situations. While few would balk if American immigrants from Russia or Cuba were described as using two *languages* in various situations, there is substantial resistance to describing African-Americans, for example, as bilingual in English and the now-infamous "Ebonics".[8]

---

6   Tobin 1994 argues persuasively for a semantic analysis of the difference between contracted and uncontracted forms. This analysis subsumes any apparent stylistic differences (which Tobin calls "incorrect and unfeasible") under the feature "±semantic integrality." While this account explains some particularly troubling examples, I am not convinced that it allows us to write register and style out of the picture completely.

7   It would not cover the peripheral instances mentioned above, or the position of dialects and various standards (a considerable problem in English, for example). Nor would it address the fact that two registers are inadequate to describe the variety of communication styles found in many modern languages.

8   For a recapitulation of the issue, see Milroy and Milroy 1999:97. The controversy began in 1996, when U.S. newspapers splashed across their front pages a story about a new curricular addition in Oakland, California: "Ebonics," defined as the language of African-Americans, which would be both used for instruction and contrasted to the study of standard English. The resulting furor, with scholars and laymen both savagely attacking

If scholars are unable, for linguistic or cultural reasons, to accept the use of the term *language* for varieties like Ebonics, the term *code* is fortuitous in that it is less provocative and allows for a closer degree of relation between the two varieties. The fact is that first- and second-generation Russian- and Spanish-speaking immigrants to the U.S. do have something in common with certain African-American communities: their use of two distinct varieties of speech in their everyday life, each of which exhibits numerous formal characteristics differentiating it from the other, and a set of situations that prompt the use of one or another variety. We can therefore draw parallels by calling all the varieties *codes*, and saying that what occurs is a form of *code-switching*.

One difficulty with code-switching is the breadth of the definition. If we declare that changes in situation can prompt switches from one code to another, we must then define precisely what a *change in situation* is. One, narrower definition of code-switching defines *situation* strictly as the overall environment in which the act takes place. In this account, code-switching occurs when, for instance, a group of teenagers hanging out in the school corridor is interrupted by the principal. The situation has changed from an informal conversation to a semi-official one, and from one between equals to one where a clear rank system is in evidence. In certain communities, the students may in fact be using a completely different language — or a different variety of a language — among themselves from the one they would use in a more official situation. Numerous different names have been proposed for this sort of switching, but following Richard Hudson (1980) and others, I will call this *situational code-switching*. Based on the definition, then, we would expect situational code-switching to be characterized by stretches of speech (or writing) in a single code, followed by a switch to a different code in response to a changed environment.

A broader definition of code-switching treats *changes in situation* more liberally, noting that a reference to a more formal item in an informal conversation may prompt a code switch, as can a sudden desire on the part of one participant to change — even momentarily — the tenor of discourse by, for example, introducing a note of seriousness or humor. In this account, a teacher might switch back and forth between a higher and lower code with a student, depending on whether he was trying to create a feeling of familiarity or present himself as a representative of authority. Richard Hudson terms this *communicative code-*

---

the dignity of this new language and fiercely defending its legitimate, separate identity, was no doubt bewildering to the Oakland Board of Education, which had in fact proposed a much more modest plan of occasional reference to African-American speech patterns in helping children to learn standard English. The very acts of *naming* this new variety of English, of terming it a *language*, and of referring to *translation* between English and Ebonics were undoubtedly among the triggers for the outpouring of feeling both for and against Ebonics. The parallels between the Czech language situation and the Ebonics debate are more extensive than appears at first blush. Alan Timberlake (UC-Berkeley) has suggested (personal communication, 1998) that many of the emotions and issues that surfaced in the Ebonics controversy have their parallels in the Standard–Common Czech divide, while Laura Janda (UNC-Chapel Hill) has sketched the numerous formal parallels between the two language systems — English/Ebonics and Standard/Common Czech — in a series of lectures reported in *Czech Language News*, Fall 1997, number 9).

*switching*, and it can be characterized by rapid changes in code, up to several times in a sentence.

A second problem with code-switching is that the term itself is controversial. The word *switch* implies a change from one discrete state to another: we *switch* a light on or off, or *switch* television channels. "Code-switching" can thus imply that at all times we are fully in one code or the other, and at certain junctures we effect a transfer over to a different code. Any token characteristic of a particular code marks us as being "in" that code. Thanks to its familiarity and long history, the term continues to be used, although many scholars now use terms like *code alternation* or *code mixing* to avoid the implications of the word *switch*.

These problems are somewhat less acute in Czech. The terminology originated in the English-language research community and much of the original research concerned English-using bilinguals. Its literal Czech equivalent *přepínání kódů* 'switching of codes' does not appear to have become as firmly established, and alongside it the terms *míšení kódů* 'mixing of codes' and *střídání kódů* 'alternation of codes' are used (see in particular Müllerová and Hoffmannová 1997, where all three terms appear, and articles by Sgall, which favor the third term.)[9]

In the received view of Bohemian Czech, two varieties are classified as *high* and *low codes*. Traditionally they were said to switch situationally (a diglossic description; see below), but more recent research suggests they in fact switch communicatively as well. There is also evidence that switching may take place even more frequently, in contexts where no change in communication can realistically be detected. This has implications for whether we accept the use of the term *code-switching* for what goes on in Czech or prefer one of the alternatives, such as *code mixing* or *code alternation*.

## 1.4. Diglossia

Ferguson 1959 noted the existence of a particular type of pervasive, formalized situational code-switching in which a single language has varieties sharply delimited by their perceived suitability across the gamut of communicative situations. A set of characteristics common to all these languages describes each language's varieties and the varieties' relationship to each other. Among these characteristics are the following: there is one variety recognizable as "high" and one as "low," with the high variety enjoying a prestige and literary heritage lacking in the low variety; the high variety is not spoken by anyone as a native dialect, but is learned exclusively through formal instruction; the varieties are suppletive[10] in the sense that in a vast majority of situations only one variety can be used, and the use of the wrong variety prompts scorn or discomfort; the high variety has codified standards, while the low variety may have generally accepted norms but lacks codified standards; the varieties together constitute a single phonological structure; the grammar of the low variety is usually a reduced version of that found in the high variety; the diglossia is relatively stable, persisting over centuries. Ferguson based his definitions on four models: Literary Arabic, which coexists

---

[9] I first became aware of the crucial differences between English and Czech terminology thanks to a series of discussions with Petr Sgall.

[10] My term, not Ferguson's.

with its many modern spoken descendants across North Africa and the Middle East; Standard
German and Swiss German; Modern Greek, standardized in the early nineteenth century, and
the spoken dialects of Greece; and Standard French, which coexists in Haiti with various
dialects of Haitian Creole.[11]

Later research on diglossia vastly expanded the scope of the term. Languages such as
Spanish and Guarani in Paraguay, French and Russian in nineteenth-century Russia, and
English in combination with numerous unrelated indigenous and immigrant languages are all
cited by Fishman as participating in diglossic relations (1980:4-7).[12] This expansion in one
sense eviscerates Ferguson's original concept in that it strips away the entire description of
the genetic relationship between the two varieties, but its advantage is that it allows certain
sociological and sociolinguistic parallels to be drawn between Fergusonian diglossic
situations and other, similar ones involving unrelated languages. In doing so, it opens the way
for linguistic analysis of how languages in a diglossic relationship are used in speech and
writing.

Much of Ferguson's analysis will at first blush seem applicable to Czech, and the
appropriateness of this designation will be treated at greater length in 3.3. After a brief
description of conventions employed in this monograph, we will turn our attention to the
specifics of variation in Czech and how to classify it.

## 1.5. Conventions and notation

In the hope of making this monograph accessible to both specialists in Czech and those
general linguists interested in the specifics of the Czech language situation, I will adhere to
somewhat eclectic conventions that draw on both traditions.

In discussions of *phonology* I will use IPA symbols in accordance with the description of
Czech found in the latest edition of the IPA Handbook (Dankovičová 1999). Pronunciation of
actual segments will be bracketed []; references to phonemes or to a typical interpretation of a
graphic rendition will be contained in slashes / /. Where necessary, I have made discussions
of the scholarly literature, much of which uses standard Czech orthography for its
transcriptions, conform to this IPA transcription. A table showing how the Czech writing
sytem maps onto an IPA description of the phonology is given in appendix 1.

Traditional Bohemistic studies have used a shorthand for referring to the different
positions in the word in which phonemic variation occurs. I have retained these notations but
have in addition introduced a system of alphanumeric labels in the charts, given below and
repeated in the appendices. My hope is that Bohemists will be able to use the Czech terms to
wade quickly through the data, while non-Bohemists may find the labels to be convenient

---

11   Since Ferguson's article was written, developments in language standardization have
     rendered two of these cases far less clearcut. A written standard based on the Greek
     demotic has gained widespread official currency in Greece, while use of the older
     *katharevousa* standard has receded (Cochran 1997). In addition, Creole has become more
     widely used in Haiti as a written language.

12   At points in Fishman's analysis I have the distinct impression he finds these examples of
     unrelated diglossia more interesting than the sort Ferguson originally described.

abstract notations for the features. The alphanumeric labels for features are not always used in the text, so as to avoid a surfeit of symbols.

**Chart 1.5.1. Labels for phonemic variation**

| Alphanumeric label | Description | Conventional notation | | |
|---|---|---|---|---|
| **Type D:** | /eː/ = /iː/ | H *é* /eː/ | = | L *ý, í* /iː/ |
| **Subtype D1:** | desinence-final | H *-é* /-eː/ | = | L *-ý, -í* /-iː/ |
| **Subtype D2:** | desinence-initial | H *-éC* /-eːC/ | = | L *-ýC, -íC* /iːC/ |
| **Subtype D3:** | word roots | H *-é-* /-eː-/ | = | L *-ý-, -í-* /-iː-/ |
| | | | | |
| **Type E:** | /iː/ = /ɛj/ | H *ý* /iː/ | = | L *ej* /ɛj/ |
| **Subtype E1:** | desinence-final | H *-ý* /-iː/ | = | L *-e* /-ɛj/ |
| **Subtype E2:** | desinence-initial | H *-ýC* /-iːC/ | = | L *-ejC* /-ɛjC/ |
| **Subtype E3:** | word roots | H *-ý-* /-iː-/ | = | L *-ej-* /-ɛj-/ |
| | | | | |
| **Type F:** | /o/ = /vo/ | H *#o* /o/ | = | L *#vo* /vo/ |
| **Subtype F1:** | word-initial | H *#o* /#o/ | = | L *#vo* /#vo/ |
| **Subtype F2:** | root-initial, word-internal | H *%o* /%o/ | = | L *%vo* /%vo/ |
| | | | | |
| **Type G:** | /uː/ = /ou/ | H *#ú* /#uː/ | = | L *#ou* /#ou/ |
| **Subtype G1:** | word-initial | H *#ú* /#uː/ | = | L *#ou* /#ou/ |
| **Subtype G2:** | root-initial, word-internal | H *%ú* /%uː/ | = | L *%ou* /%ou/ |

H = "high" code, Standard Czech (see below); L = "low" code, Common Czech (see below).

In discussing morphological, syntactic and lexical features, I chose to leave items in standard Czech orthography, although I offer some IPA equivalents in the first major table of features (chart 2.3.1).

*Morphological features* under discussion are indicated in one of two ways. For Bohemists, each feature is indicated by a "low code" instantiation of the feature; thus, *dobrý auta* is used as a shorthand for all examples of nominative plural levelling in the neuter forms of adjectives (the "high" variant would be *dobrá auta*; see 2.4). For ease of reference for scholars not familiar with Czech, each feature has also been assigned a number referenced in appendix 2. A similar cataloguing system is offered for *syntactic features*, and repeated in appendix 4.

*Glosses and translations* are offered for all material. *Intralinear translations* are additionally provided when relevant to the discussion. Otherwise, only *ordinary translations* are given, with the feature in question printed in bold type.

## 2. The Czech language situation

There is a long tradition of interest in the peculiar language situation that has arisen in the Czech lands. Several excellent reviews of the situation and the history of research on it are available in English (respectively Dickins 1995 and Gammelgaard 1999; see also Townsend 1990 for a description of Prague Czech and Sgall et al. 1992 for a detailed examination of the problem), as well as in Czech (see bibliography).

### 2.1. Historical background

What we call Standard or Literary Czech (*spisovná čeština*, hereafter SC) is not a straightforward case of a written variety that developed out of a spoken variety.[13] After roughly three centuries of prosperity as a written language, Czech declined in use following 1620. While writing in Czech was not completely extinguished, the Czech literary language lost influence and prestige and was largely supplanted by German.[14] Czech, of course, continued to be spoken, and numerous developments in the spoken language (some traceable to increased German influence during that period, others the result of preexisting trends in the language) are attested over the next century and a half.

During the National Revival (*národní obrození*) in the mid-nineteenth century, a group of leading intellectuals began to promote Czech again as a national written language. There was much discussion over whether to look to current speech for their models, or to draw instead on the "golden age" of Czech prose: the era of the Kralice Bible, translated by the Moravian Brethren in the 1580s. The latter view prevailed. This new standard, then, was not intended as a written analogue to spoken Czech; instead, it was meant to replace German in certain kinds of discourse with a codified, authoritative variety of the local language. Further moves during the nineteenth and early twentieth century to "purify" the language by removing real or perceived Germanisms only increased the divide between ordinary spoken Czech and the written standard (see Thomas 1996a and 1996b, Gammelgaard 1999).

The mid- and late twentieth century witnessed a certain rapprochement between the standard variety and the spoken language. The Czech Language Institute (*Ústav pro jazyk český*), which in the postwar period has been charged with propagating and regulating language norms, has, under the influence of Prague School functionalism, distanced itself from the purist, conservative position of the journal *Naše řeč* ('Our Language') in the interwar period, taking the position that certain accommodations must be made within SC to admit

---

[13] Discussion of the historical and cultural factors surrounding the rise of modern Czech can be found in Auty 1976.

[14] The commonly held belief that Czech "died out" completely as a written language is not, in fact, supported by historical research. See Stich 1987.

some non-SC variants.[15] Much credit belongs to the eminent Czech linguist Havránek, who in the 1930s was already pushing for scholarly attention to a second unofficial variety of Bohemian Czech used in speech (now usually called *obecná čeština* 'Common Czech', hereafter CC) and tried to assess both its nature and its relationship to the literary standard.[16] It was Havránek who, in this second vein, first posited the existence of a spoken standard code, "Colloquial Czech (*hovorová čeština*)."

In this spirit of guarded rapprochement between a codified standard and the uncodified spoken varieties, a number of official changes have been made in the postwar period. These pronouncements from the Czech Language Institute have legitimized the use in SC of certain formerly non-SC forms, such as *třech* 'three (genitive plural)' or *pracuju* 'I work', which are now found alongside traditional SC forms like *tří* and *pracuji* (but see 3.2 below). They have been accompanied by orthographic reforms that aim to bring the writing system into line with current pronunciation. These moves have lessened the differences between the standard and spoken varieties, but the lines dividing the standard from other varieties of the language are still numerous and deeply felt.[17]

## 2.2. Synchronic background

We can summarize the questions pertinent to our discussion of contemporary Czech as follows: 1) How do native speakers of Czech acquire SC? 2) How does SC relate to the spoken varieties of Czech? 3) In what situations are these varieties used?

Everyone, regardless of social class, is raised speaking a dialect whose phonology, morphology, syntax and lexicon differ substantially from those of SC. The variants marked specifically as SC do not occur as a group in anyone's native dialect, at least not in Bohemia; rather, SC variants are acquired alongside native variants, but starting at a later age and at first in more limited contexts. Czech speakers will hear SC from an early age on television and when read to; they begin to acquire an active knowledge of SC when they start school at age 6, and use it primarily in the course of their education.[18] They write using SC and read SC,

---

15  For a different perspective on the role of the Prague School, see Starý 1993, which examines reactionary and conservative elements in Prague functionalism.

16  In a series of heated exchanges with Sgall in the early 1960s, however, Havránek and his colleagues repudiated any wholesale attempt to codify features considered specific to spoken Czech and legitimize their use in SC, showing that there was a limit to their tolerance. See Bělič et al. 1962, Sgall 1960, 1962.

17  Nebeská 1996 is an insightful analysis of the development of standards and norms in Czech. Gammelgaard 1999 contains an excellent, concise account of the different schools of thought in the postwar period. For a more complete discussion of purism and its effects see Thomas 1991.

18  Sgall states: "Even today, there are practically no native speakers of Standard Czech, since most children get acquainted with this code just in a passive way, watching TV, listening to the nurses and teachers in kindergartens, and partly to the overcareful speech

and most of the television they watch makes use of SC. Films and plays employ SC, as do public speakers, teachers and journalists, although non-SC forms are increasingly heard in these formal situations.[19] In almost all other contexts, Czechs will use their native dialect or some modified form of it, sometimes mixing it with SC or alternating between their native dialect and SC.[20] Virtually no one in Bohemia, no matter how learned and erudite, speaks SC at home with his family.

The nature of this "native dialect" has proved to be elusive and contentious. A large percentage of the population grows up speaking the variety termed *Common Czech* (*obecná čeština*). CC, which developed from a strictly local dialect, also functions as an interdialect.[21] For all intents and purposes, it has supplanted the local dialects of Central Bohemia from which it evolved, and in this capacity is spoken by more than a quarter of the Czech Republic's population of 10 million. CC is widely used elsewhere in the Czech Republic as well. In towns and urban centers throughout Bohemia it is well on its way to completely replacing local dialects. Throughout Bohemia, in fact, the historical dialects as language systems are being relegated to the fringes of language use (among the elderly and in geographically peripheral regions).[22] If all of Bohemia and the border regions of Moravia are included in the CC speech area, then CC can be said to be the native dialect of upwards of 60 percent of the Czech population (see figure 2.2.1).

---

of their mothers addressing them. The active use of the Standard is as a rule acquired only at school." (1994:140)

[19] For a condemnation of such widespread practices and the "low level of professionality" (*jde většinou o nízkou profesionalitu*) they evoke for certain listeners, see Uličný 1995:23-25.

[20] Chloupek 1987 gives just a few examples from the borderline between "written" and "spoken" communication: "a mother leaving an improvised message on a scrap of paper for her family, a television discussion on a specialized subject where those taking part...adopt a more exclusive vocabulary, or again the taped spoken language, relatively permanent. Which language quality (written or spoken) will dominate for example, in the speech of an experienced teacher who, almost certainly from memory, presents to his pupils knowledge gained from textbooks, that is, from written texts?" (98)

[21] Here I use "interdialect" in the sense proposed in Sgall et al. 1992: a former regional dialect, minus some more obvious regional features, which gains currency as a koine or neutral variety outside its source area. There are variations in CC as it is spoken outside its central Bohemian heartland, but these are for the most part minor.

[22] Some regional features do survive, but arguably as regional variations of CC. The account in this paragraph condenses information found in Hronek 1972:111-118 and Sgall (various). These accounts appear to be impressionistic, rather than being based on comprehensive surveys of language use, which until recently were scarce. More surveys of local language use have been forthcoming in the last few years, and eventually a larger picture of the relationships between Czech dialects and interdialects should be available.

**Figure 2.2.1. Schematic map of the Czech Republic**

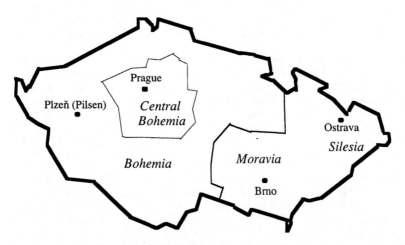

The situation in Moravia is more complex. Some parts of western Moravia are within the CC sphere. In addition, at least three native interdialects or major dialect groups can be found on Moravian territory, as well as numerous smaller dialects.[23] *Haná*, the most widespread, is found in central and northern Moravia. *Silesian* and *Slovácko* subsume old dialect groups that are transitional, respectively, to Polish and Slovak, and are found in the northeast and southeast of the country. CC is also said to be making inroads into traditional speech patterns in the larger Moravian cities. Moravian scholars, however, have frequently denied that CC is acceptable as a neutral spoken code in Moravia; far more common, they say, is the use of a modified version of SC (i.e. the elusive *hovorová čeština* 'Colloquial Czech' discussed in 3.8).[24]

Given the disagreements over when and where SC and CC are used, it is problematic even to decide what to call them. We can take refuge in standard sociolinguistic terminology and call them *codes (kódy)*, but this may imply accepting certain other models, such as code-switching, that will prove problematic later on. Other terms such as *levels (vrstvy)* and *styles (styly)* carry equally heavy implications. The most neutral Czech term is Havránek's *jazykový*

---

23 The question of whether these three categories constitute interdialects with minor regional variants or dialect groups is of crucial importance in establishing the relationship between SC and spoken Czech in Moravia. Some Moravian scholars have insisted on the lack of an interdialectal mode of communication for Moravian speakers (see below and 3.8).

24 See, for example, Davidová et al. 1997. We can nonetheless dispense with the notion that Moravian dialects are generally more "standard" (*spisovný*) than Bohemian dialects, an old wives' tale that has wide currency among non-philologists in the Czech Republic.

*útvar*, roughly 'language formation', which is cumbersome in English; hence I use the more economical and noncommittal term *variety*, following Ferguson (1994:23-24) and others.[25]

In this study I will concentrate on the linguistic situation in Bohemia and the CC-speaking parts of Moravia. The situation elsewhere in Moravia and in Silesia, while having serious implications for language planning and questions of national identity, will remain outside the scope of this work.

It will be evident from this description that the Czech language situation is markedly different from those usually used in discussing standard languages and spoken languages. Many diglossic communities constitute a minor or insignificant portion of the community using the standard language — a claim that could be made for the Haitians with respect to French, the Swiss with respect to German, or the population of any single Arabic-speaking country considered against the entire Arabic-using world, but one which is clearly not valid for the Bohemians with respect to Czech. Bohemia is the dominant economic, cultural and political force of the Czech Republic, and contains more than half the nation's population and territory. One close and well-studied parallel to Czech can be found in Sinhala, the language of Sri Lanka, which has an indigenous H and L variety with a similar relationship and distribution to that of Czech.[26] Also similar are Greek and Norwegian, although both these languages have developed alternative standards closer to the demotic dialects, at once lessening the diglossic character of these languages while complicating the language situation further (Cochran 1997, Håkon and Janicki 1995). Nor is the situation exactly parallel to those linguistically separate nations coexisting within larger political entities with a different standard, such as the Alsatians within France (Gardner-Chloros 1995), the East African use of Swahili as a *lingua franca* or immigrant groups in the United States. In these situations, the boundaries between the two codes should in theory be clearly marked, while in Czech the two varieties share a large enough percentage of vocabulary, phonology, morphology and syntax that many utterances cannot clearly be assigned to one or the other variety.

Given these facts, it is substantially more difficult to approach the Czech language situation from the point of view of *oppression, social exclusion* and *ethnic conflict*. If the varied nature of Czech is a tool of oppression, then it is an oppression inflicted willingly by the majority of speakers upon themselves; if it excludes socially, then it does so as perniciously as any society that places a high value on education; and, since the Czech Republic is an independent, ethnically highly homogeneous nation (upwards of 95 percent of the population identifies as ethnically Czech, Moravian or Silesian[27]), the ethnic conflict card

---

[25]  Ferguson (1994:23) states that: "Sets of identifying markers of dialect, register, and genre variation vary greatly in the degree of cohesiveness they show as systems and the sharpness of the boundaries between them; *the more cohesive the systems, the sharper the boundaries, and the more they are perceived by the participants as separate entities, the more useful it is to analyze them as language varieties: dialects, registers and genres, respectively.*" (Italics original.)

[26]  Sinhala is examined in Paolillo 1997.

[27]  See Hlavsová 1997:185. Before the Czecho-Slovak Federal Republic was dissolved on 1 January 1993, the 10 million Czechs coexisted in a single federal state with their 5 million neighbors in the Slovak Republic (mostly ethnic Slovaks, the remainder being Romany,

has little value in the current climate. If anything, the existence of a supradialectal national standard equalizes differences between the Czech regions, by putting all native speakers of Czech at an equal disadvantage and presenting them with the visual appearance of a common language.[28] Lacking the strong politicizing influences present in so many language situations, Czech in many ways offers an ideal context in which to examine the interaction between two coexisting varieties.

### 2.3. How different are Standard and Common Czech?

Thorough and lucid English-language descriptions of the differences between CC and SC can be found in Dickins 1995, Townsend 1990 and Sgall et al. 1992, among others, as well as in several Czech-language sources. The system described briefly hereafter represents what I will call the "received view" of Czech.

Two codes, SC and CC, are systematically distinguished on a number of levels. They have overlapping but not identical morphological inventories, inventories of syntactic constructions, and lexicons. They share a phonemic inventory, although the distribution of these phonemes is different (see below). While many works make no distinction between these levels, others give primacy to phonology and morphology as the clearest markers of the SC–CC distinction, or to one of them. The differences are sketched in Table 2.3.1. (Labels are given in alphabetical and numerical order in the appendices. Unlabeled items were not tracked in the corpus, or were tracked and found in such small numbers that they were not reported in the discussions in chapter 5.)

---

Carpathians and Hungarians). However, the position of Czech prior to 1993 was arguably not that different. Each of the CSFR's two constituent republics had its own official language, and all business within each republic was conducted in that republic's language. Czech and Slovak are similar enough to allow for a more or less automatic passive bilingualism, so the primary difference after 1992 in the Czech Republic has been a significant curtailment in the amount of Slovak heard on television and radio and seen in print. The effects have been more noticeable in the Slovak Republic, where Czech had a more pervasive presence.

28  The situation does make learning Czech substantially harder for the Czech Republic's non-Czech-speaking minority communities, which include: a substantial Romany population long resident in the Czech and Slovak Republics; workers and refugees from Vietnam, the former Yugoslavia and the former Soviet Union; and largely transient communities composed of citizens of wealthy western nations. (As Hlavsová 1995 notes, it has proved extremely difficult to count non-citizens, and there is reason to believe that the Romany population has been drastically undercounted.) However, it is safe to say that communities rarely engage in linguistic engineering solely to make their language more convenient to learn for non-speakers, resident or otherwise.

**Chart 2.3.1. Distinguishing features of SC and CC**

| Feature | Lab. | SC | CC |
|---|---|---|---|
| ***phoneme distribution*** | | | |
| *original front long vowels* | D, E | *é* [ɛː], *ý* [iː], *í* [iː] | *í* [iː], *ej* [ɛj] |
| *original vowels word-initially or root-initially* | F, G | #*ú* [uː], #*o* [o] | #*ou* [ou], #*vo* [vo] |
| *certain consonant clusters* | -- | permitted | may be simplified |
| *vowels in some word roots and some desinences* | -- | long | may be shortened to varying degrees |
| *vowels in some emphatic/ strongly emotional words* | -- | short | may be lengthened to varying degrees |
| ***morphological inventory*** | | | |
| *nominative plural form of adjectives* | 3, 4 | 3 distinct forms: neuter; masculine animate; masculine inanimate/feminine | only one form, derived from the masculine inanimate & feminine form |
| *masculine/neuter locative & instrumental singular of adjectives* | 15 | 2 distinct forms | only one form (occasionally with shortened vowel) |
| *instrumental plural of adjectives and nouns, all genders, most declension patterns* | 10 | masculine/neuter nouns: *y* or *i*, pronounced [ɪ]; feminine nouns: -*ami*, -*emi* [amɪ, ɛmɪ]; adjectives: -*ými* or -*ími* , pronounced [iːmɪ] | nouns, all genders: -*ama*, -*ema* [ama, ɛma] adjectives: -*ejma*, -*íma* [ɛjma, iːma] |
| *nominative plural of masculine animate nouns* | 6 | -*i*, -*é*, -*ové* [ɪ, ɛː, ovɛː] | -*i*, -*ové* [ɪ,  ovɛː] (SC -*é* = CC -*i*) |
| *3rd person plural of the non-past tense* | 13, 16 | -*í* or -*ejí* [iː, ɛjiː]  -*ají* [ajiː] | -*ej* [ɛj] only (or -*í* [iː] only in certain regions) -*aj* [aj] |

| Feature | Lab. | SC | CC |
|---------|------|----|----|
| *past participle of C-stem verbs*[29] | 9 | *řízl, nesl* <br> -Cl | *říznul, nes* <br> -Cnul, -C |
| *conditional auxiliary verb (1st person, singular and plural)* | 1, 2 | *bych,* <br> *bychom* | *bysem* (Central Bohemia), <br> *bysme* |
| *1st person singular and 3rd person plural of the non-past tense (verbs with a stem ending in a velar)* | 7, 8 | *mohu, můžeš....mohou* <br> [-Ku, -Kou vs. -ČɛC] <br> stem-final velar retained <br> before back vowels | *můžu, můžeš...můžou* <br> [-Ču, -ČɛC, -Čou] <br> Č before front & back vowels <br> (permitted for some SC) |
| *1st person singular and 3rd person plural of the non-past tense (verbs with a stem ending in a soft consonant)* | 11, 12 | 1. sg. *pracuji* [-jɪ] <br> 3. pl. *pracují* [-jiː] | 1. sg. *pracuju* [-ju] <br> 3. pl. *pracujou* [-jou] <br> (permitted for some SC) |
| *1st person plural of the non-past tense (with -e-theme vowel)* [30] | 17 | *vedeme* <br> (with final [ɛ]) | *vedem* <br> (no final [ɛ]) |
| *infinitives of verbs with a consonantal stem* | 14 | *říci* (ends in [t͡sɪ]) | *říct* (ends in [t͡st]) <br> (permitted for most SC) |

---

[29] Gammelgaard (personal communication) notes that the deletion of final /l/ in consonantal-stem verbs has a special status in Czech; it was regularly used in poetry in the late nineteenth and early- to mid-twentieth century, and thus is not entirely CC. I would further suggest that the use of the bare-stem form was probably closely tied to rhyme and meter, given that the final /l/ is syllabic. However, modern grammars such as the *Příruční mluvnice češtiny* (hereafter PMČ) no longer list the bare stem as an alternate acceptable form, calling it instead a "regional substandard form" (326). Usage of this form outside poetic contexts apparently does not ordinarily evoke the older, poetic function.

[30] Sgall (personal communication) has pointed out the use of the so-called CC forms like *vedem* in poetry and nineteenth-century prose, which indicates that these forms have a well-established literary pedigree. Here again, however, the poetic function is likely to be metric, and such forms are considered substandard in ordinary modern prose (PMČ 313), warranting their inclusion in this chart.

| *Feature* | Lab. | SC | CC |
|-----------|------|----|----|
| ***syntactic features*** | | | |
| *relative pronouns* | 1 | *který, jenž* (agree with referent) | *k(t)erej* (agrees with referent), *co* (invariable, see 5.3) |
| *predicate nominals* | 3 | found in nominative or instrumental case | found only in nominative case |
| *vocative case* | -- | all parts of a compound noun decline | only title declines |
| *subject pronouns* | -- | for emphasis, contrast | used regularly |
| *subject reduplication* | 4 | not permitted | frequent with forms of *von* |
| *past tense auxiliary* | 5 | obligatory in 1st and 2nd person forms | frequently dropped in 1st person singular, especially for contrast |
| *adjective forms* | -- | short and long forms of adjectives used predicatively for nominative and accusative cases; long forms describe permanent, unqualified states, short forms describe temporary or qualified states. | short forms only as relics; else long forms found everywhere. |
| *deictic adjectives* | -- | *ten, tento, tamten* | *ten, tamten, tenhle, tenhleten, tamhleten,* etc. |
| ***lexicon*** | | (numerous words exclusive to SC; other SC words can be used in CC but also have exclusively CC synonyms) | (numerous words exclusive to CC; other CC words are admissible in SC but also have exclusively SC synonyms) |

This lengthy catalogue of differences must be set against a far longer list of features and items that the two varieties share. Havránek (1963:258) pointed out that while the differences in adjectival flexion are profound, in verbal flexion, for instance, roughly 90 percent of forms are shared between the two varieties, with only 10 percent having distinct SC and CC forms. Overlaps between the two varieties will be discussed further in sections 2.4 and 5.0.

## 2.4. Outline of Czech

A brief explanation of some of the features listed in chart 2.3.1 may be helpful for those not familiar with Czech. (Those familiar with Czech may wish to skip ahead to chapter 3.)

Czech, a member of the Slavic branch of Indo-European, has a vocalic system based on short and long vowels that occur freely in any syllable.[31] The language has phonological word stress, which is fixed on the first syllable and is considered to be relatively weak; there is no vowel reduction or neutralization in unstressed syllables, and no concomitant lengthening of vowels under stress.

The vowel inventory consists of five short vowels, five long vowels, and seven glide diphthongs. Short and long vowels have the same character, being differentiated primarily by the duration of the vowel (although there is a distinguishable difference between the short high front vowel and the long high front vowel, which is noticeably higher).

**Chart 2.4.1. Vowel inventory of SC and CC[32]**

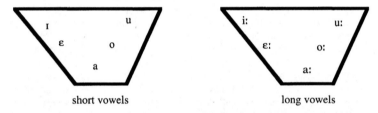

short vowels          long vowels

The glide diphthongs are /aj/, /ɛj/, /oj/, /uj/, /au/, /ɛu/, /ou/. The primary difference between SC and CC is in the distribution of these vocalic phonemes and diphthongs. Some (like /oː/, /au/, /oj/, /eu/ are found primarily with borrowings in both SC and CC. Others, like /ɛː/, have that status in CC but are common in SC, and still others, like /ɛj/, have a restricted distribution in SC but a much wider occurrence in CC.

This distributional difference is realized in a number of ways. For example: many word stems occur with two vocalic variants, one a short vowel and the other a long vowel or diphthong. In SC the short vowel *y*, representing /ɪ/, often alternates with the long vowel *ý*, representing /iː/, in the same stem. In CC that same short vowel /ɪ/ is said to alternate instead with /ɛj/ in many of those contexts, e.g. SC *vymluvit–výmluva* 'to excuse–an excuse', *pohybovat–hýbat* 'move' vs. CC *vymluvit–vejmluva, pohybovat–hejbat*. By contrast, in SC the diphthong /ɛj/ is relatively restricted, occurring primarily as an imperative ending and in the nominative singular ending of some nouns (*trofej, kolej*, etc.), contexts in which it is also found in CC. Further discussion of Czech phonology can be found in Kučera 1961, Townsend 1990, and various grammars.

---

[31]  The consonantal inventory is listed in appendix 1.

[32]  cf. Townsend 1990:24, Dankovičová 1999:72.

Differences in realization of consonantal phonemes are sporadic and center on the simplification of consonant clusters. The inventory of consonants is the same for SC as CC, although CC may have a reduced number and variety of consonant clusters, with constraints that are missing in SC, e.g. the lack of initial consonant clusters like /vʒd/, /jd/, /tʃt/.

Czech, like other Slavic languages, is highly inflected. It has three *genders* (masculine, feminine, neuter) and a *subgender* traditionally called "masculine animate" encompassing those nouns of masculine grammatical gender that describe humans, animals and anthropomorphized beings. (Nouns that are grammatically feminine and neuter in gender do not have separate animate and inanimate subgenders.) Nouns have *singular* and *plural* forms (and, in rare instances, special *dual* forms for indicating objects typically found in pairs) for each of seven traditionally distinguished *cases* (nominative, genitive, dative, accusative, vocative, locative and instrumental) that indicate syntactic relations.[33] Number, gender and case are indicated by *portmanteau morphs* suffixed to the stem; that is, each ending may mark any combination of gender, subgender and number but cannot be analyzed further into constituent morphemes representing gender, subgender or number individually. Each noun has thirteen potential forms, and declines according to one of a dozen or so major or numerous minor *paradigms* that correspond with their gender and subgender assignments. In practice there is a fair amount of *syncretism* within nominal paradigms, with some forms doing duty for two or three cases.

Adjectives also decline and agree in number and gender with the nouns they modify. There are two basic adjective declensions, plus possessive adjectives (e.g. *můj* 'my', *náš* 'our') and personal adjectives (e.g. *matčin* 'mother's', *Havlův* 'Havel's'); some of the most common adjectives — *ten* 'this', *jeden* 'one', *všechen* 'all' — do not follow the basic paradigms. Pronouns decline as well.

Czech verbs have two stems, one used for forming the non-past tense and the imperative mood, the other for forming the past participle and the infinitive. In the *indicative mood*, the *non-past tense* can have present or future meaning, depending on the verb concerned and the context in which it is used; to the stem is added a portmanteau morph combining attributes of number (singular or plural) and person (first, second or third), giving six forms. The *past tense* consists of a participle that agrees with the subject in number and gender, and an auxiliary verb — the appropriate non-past form of the verb *být* 'be' — that appears in the first and second persons. Some verbs (those of imperfective aspect) have a distinct periphrastic future tense as well. SC admits a periphrastic *past conditional tense* not found in the spoken language. There is a *conditional mood*, where a special conditional auxiliary is used with the past-tense participle, and an *imperative mood*.

This array of tenses and moods coexists with a system of *aspect* based around pairs or groups of verbs with similar meanings (usually formed from a single root by suffixation and/or prefixation). For conjugation, verbs are said to fall into six traditional *classes* and several *subclasses* that indicate which theme vowel and desinences are used, as well as whether consonant and vowel mutations are applied to either stem in conjugation.

---

[33]   The vocative is usually said to stand outside syntactic relationships, and its status as a case is therefore problematic. Distinct vocative forms exist only for singular nouns; for adjectives and plural nouns, the vocative is identical to the nominative case.

Although the majority of forms are common to the spoken and the written varieties of Czech, there are numerous points in the system where two forms are distinguished. In many instances one form is said to be SC, the other CC. The tables below present an overview of the phonological and morphological variants, in a vastly simplified form. SC–CC differences said to be phonological in nature are <u>underlined</u>; differences said to be morphological are in **bold**. The SC form precedes the CC form, separated by a slash. For the sake of economy, only the part of the word where variation occurs is given. For instance, the notation "dobr-ý/ej" means that the SC form is *dobrý* and the CC form is *dobrej*, as the variant endings ý and ej are attached to the part of the word (*dobr*) preceding the dash.

I call the system presented here "vastly simplified" because it implies a stylistic and functional unity between all forms marked as SC and between all those marked as CC. Such a unity is not reflected in contemporary usage, as we will see later; the point is to show the pervasiveness of stylistically differentiated doublets in parts of the Czech inflectional system.

In a sense, however, as Gammelgaard has noted (personal communication), the paradigms that follow also show the extent to which Czech inflection is a single system, albeit one with some systematic register differentiation. Noun declensions are largely uniform for both varieties, as are certain verb conjugations and the soft adjectival declension (not shown).

**Chart 2.4.2. Adjectives ("hard" declension):** *dobr-ý* 'good'

| singular case | m. animate | m. inanimate | neuter | feminine |
|---|---|---|---|---|
| nominative | dobr-<u>ý/ej</u> | dobr-<u>ý/ej</u> | dobr-<u>é/ý</u> | dobr-á |
| genitive | dobr-<u>ého/ýho</u> | dobr-<u>ého/ýho</u> | dobr-<u>ého/ýho</u> | dobr-<u>é/ý</u> |
| dative | dobr-<u>ému/ýmu</u> | dobr-<u>ému/ýmu</u> | dobr-<u>ému/ýmu</u> | dobr-<u>é/ý</u> |
| accusative | dobr-<u>ého/ýho</u> | dobr-<u>ý/ej</u> | dobr-<u>é/ý</u> | dobr-ou |
| locative | dobr-<u>ém/ým</u>/ym | dobr-<u>ém/ým</u>/ym | dobr-<u>ém/ým</u>/ym | dobr-<u>é/ý</u> |
| instrumental | dobr-**ým/ym** | dobr-**ým/ym** | dobr-**ým/ym** | dobr-ou |

| plural case | | | | |
|---|---|---|---|---|
| nominative | dob-**ří/rý** | dobr-<u>é/ý</u> | dobr-á/ý | dobr-<u>é/ý</u> |
| genitive | dobr-<u>ých/ejch</u> | dobr-<u>ých/ejch</u> | dobr-<u>ých/ejch</u> | dobr-<u>ých/ejch</u> |
| dative | dobr-<u>ým/ejm</u> | dobr-<u>ým/ejm</u> | dobr-<u>ým/ejm</u> | dobr-<u>ým/ejm</u> |
| accusative | dobr-<u>é/ý</u> | dobr-<u>é/ý</u> | dobr-á/ý | dobr-<u>é/ý</u> |
| locative | dobr-<u>ých/ejch</u> | dobr-<u>ých/ejch</u> | dobr-<u>ých/ejch</u> | dobr-<u>ých/ejch</u> |
| instrumental | dobr-<u>ými/ejma</u> | dobr-<u>ými/ejma</u> | dobr-<u>ými/ejma</u> | dobr-<u>ými/ejma</u> |

*Notes to chart 2.4.2:*
Instrumental plural variation is found with declinable adjectives of all declension patterns.

The remaining morphological variations are represented in other adjectival declensions, but phonological ones, such as the so-called 'soft' adjectival declension, are not, as the conditioning environment (the vowel /ɛː/ in the desinence) for the change was historically not present.

The vocative form of the adjective is the same as the nominative form.

**Chart 2.4.3.** Verbs (all major classes)

| traditional class<br>translation | 1 (all others)<br>'be able' | 1 (all others)<br>'lead' | 2 (-nout)<br>'slice' | 3 (-et, -ět)<br>'know how' |
|---|---|---|---|---|
| infinitive | moc-**i/t** | v<u>é</u>st/v<u>í</u>st/vest | říznout | umět |
| 1. sg. non-past | **mohu/můžu** | vedu | říznu | umím |
| 2. sg. non-past | **můžeš** | vedeš | řízneš | umíš |
| 3. sg. non-past | **může** | vede | řízne | umí |
| 1. pl. non-past | **mův-eme/em** | ved-**eme/em** | řízn-**eme/em** | umíme |
| 2. pl. non-past | **můžete** | vedete | říznete | umíte |
| 3. pl. non-past | **mohou/můžou** | vedou | říznou | um-**ějí/ěj/í** |
| past participle | **mohl/moh** | vedl/ved | říz-**l/nul** | uměl |

| traditional class<br>translation | 4 (-it)<br>'request' | 5 (-C+at)<br>'do, make' | 5 (-C+at)<br>'write' | 6 (-ovat)<br>'work' |
|---|---|---|---|---|
| infinitive | prosit | dělat | psát | pracovat |
| 1. sg. non-past | prosím | dělám | píš-**i/u** | pracuj-**u/i** |
| 2. sg. non-past | prosíš | děláš | píšeš | pracuješ |
| 3. sg. non-past | prosí | dělá | píše | pracuje |
| 1. pl. non-past | prosíme | děláme | píš-**eme/em** | pracuj-**eme/em** |
| 2. pl. non-past | prosíte | děláte | píšete | pracujete |
| 3. pl. non-past | pros-**í/ej(í)** | děl-**ají/aj** | píš-**í/ou** | pracuj-**í/ou** |
| past participle | prosil | dělal | psal | pracoval |

*Notes to chart 2.4.3:*

The classes containing *prosit* and *umět* are large although the class as a whole is unproductive.

The classes containing *dělat*, *pracovat* and *říznout* are large and productive.

The classes containing *psát* and *vést (víst, vest)* are small but contain many high-frequency verbs.

The class containing *moci (moct)* is very small. It contains only a couple of high-frequency verbs; *moci/moct*, however, is one of the most frequent verbs in the language ('can/be able').

The remaining classes all have a fair number of high-frequency verbs.

The *vést*-class infinitive has three variants: its SC form and two CC forms, one with CC /i:/ and the other with a short vowel.

In theory Czech infinitives have a further SC variant ending in *-ti* instead of just *-t*, but this is by now bookish, even archaic, and in contemporary usage is usually used to humorous effect, for deliberate archaizing, or as a citation of an older text.

**Chart 2.4.4. Nouns (four common declensions)**

| translation | masc. animate, hard stem 'Englishman' | masc. inanimate, soft stem 'machine' | feminine, hard stem 'cassette' | feminine, i-stem 'bone' |
|---|---|---|---|---|
| **singular case** | | | | |
| nominative | Angličan | stroj | kazeta | kost |
| genitive | Angličana | stroje | kazety | kosti |
| dative | Angličanovi | stroji | kazetě | kosti |
| accusative | Angličana | stroj | kazetu | kost |
| vocative | Angličane | stroji | kazeto | kosti |
| locative | Angličanovi | stroji | kazetě | kosti |
| instrumental | Angličanem | strojem | kazetou | kostí |
| **plural case** | | | | |
| nominative | Angličan-é/i | stroje | kazety | kosti |
| genitive | Angličanů | strojů | kazet | kostí |
| dative | Angličanům | strojům | kazetám | kostem |
| accusative | Angličany | stroje | kazety | kosti |
| locative | Angličanech | strojích | kazetách | kostech |
| instrumental | Angličan-y/ama | stroj-i/ema | kazet-ami/ama | kost-mi/ma |

*Notes to chart 2.4.4:*
There are many declension patterns not represented here.
The nominative plural alternation is found only in a subclass of masculine animate hard nouns.
The instrumental alternation is found throughout all declensions.
The vocative is not listed as a distinct plural case, as it always has the same form as the nominative.

# 3. The relationship between standard and non-standard forms

Charts 2.3.1 to 2.4.4 take for granted an important fact: both SC and CC can be represented in both speech and writing using ordinary Czech orthography. This fact is so obvious that it is often ignored. Many languages, Czech included, have writing systems that stabilized at an earlier stage of the language's development. Yet as the spoken language evolves, our expectations of how letters are realized in speech often evolve as well. In English — an admittedly extreme example — the letters on the page give only a rough indication of how words are currently pronounced in most standards, with each letter having multiple values depending on its graphic, phonological, morphological and lexical environment. This parallel evolution makes for a sloppy correspondence between grapheme and phoneme, but the "notional" nature of English spelling allows a single graphic shape to stand for a variety of possible pronunciations in the multiple standards of English as they evolve over time. The peculiar history of Czech has meant that this gradually evolved correspondence is lacking. When SC was created, an archaizing pronunciation for it came into existence as well, albeit one that functioned within the limits of the CC phonological system.[34] However, since the Czech alphabet contains enough graphemes to represent the phonemic inventory of CC, authors were able to use it to convey CC variants as well. Thus conventions for notating CC also came to exist. No such systematic parallel exists in the more widely studied languages of Western Europe.

An example will serve to clarify the point. English speakers would not dream of pronouncing the words *thought* or *night* with the penultimate phoneme /x/ that the spelling at one stage reflected. In fact, only the philologist is likely to be aware that *gh* ever had this value in these words. For the average speaker, the graphic representations *thought, night* correspond only to the words he says as [θɔːt], [naɪt]. But the average Czech speaker knows he is to pronounce the word *jablko* 'apple' as [jabl̩ko] when reading, and that it corresponds to the spoken word [japko], which can be written *japko* to show casualness of speech.[35] This can be diagrammed on chart 1.2.1, as seen below in chart 3.0.1.

---

[34] As seen in 2.4, the phonemic inventories of CC and SC are virtually identical. Only the glottal stop (found before word-initial vowels and between vowels on a morpheme boundary) causes some difficulty. According to the PMČ, the glottal stop is facultative in SC and non-phonemic, being a feature of segmentation and word division rather than phonology (34, 46, 48, 53-54, 59). Since it is often omitted in CC as well, and as Czech has no grapheme representing the glottal stop, this issue is pushed to the side in any examination of written Czech. CC may have slightly different constraints on consonant clusters, although many of those can be explained as allegro pronunciations that are not "acknowledged" for slower, more careful CC speech. The evolution of an archaizing pronunciation for SC did not, for example, extend to the reintroduction of distinct pronunciations for written *i* vs. *y* and *í* vs. *ý*.

[35] The impression is similar, although not identical, to that created by English spellings like *tonite, nitely, thru, cuz*, and so forth, which are meant to evoke informality but are

**Chart 3.0.1.  The word 'apple' in four realizations**

| *medium (across)* *register (down)* | *writing* | *speaking* |
|---|---|---|
| *formal, official* | jablko | [jabļko] |
| *informal, unofficial* | japko | [japko] |

This chart could be repeated across the spectrum of items in chart 2.3.1.  A thorough and illuminating exploration of the relationship between orthography, punctuation and language can be found in Gammelgaard 1997:57-119 and will not be repeated here.

## 3.1.  Exclusivity and distinctness of codes

The main claim for the distinctness of two codes, SC and CC, that are part of the same language system rests on the lack of neutral, unmarked variants at many points in a communicative situation.  Language users are forced to "declare allegiance" to a code whenever they reach one of these points.  This can happen several times in a phrase or sentence, making completely neutral discourse an impossibility.  Sgall et al. 1992 present an (artificially-constructed) example that captures the extent of the divide neatly:

3.1a  SC:  S    takový̌mi   lidmi       **bychom**   nemluvili   o    (tom)
      CC:  S    takove**jma**   lidma       **bysme**     nemluvili   **vo**    tom
           with such-**INSTR** people-**INSTR** would-**1PL.** not-speak-**PPL** **about** that-**LOC**

      SC:  tvém     byt̆e.
      CC:  tvym     byt̆e.
           your-**LOC** apartment-**LOC**

'We **wouldn't** speak **about** that apartment of **yours** with **people like them.**'

The first variant is clearly standard.  We might find it in a novel, but we would not expect to hear it under normal circumstances in a pub, unless the speaker had some purpose in choosing standard forms (see below).  The second variant is clearly a transcription of speech. We would not expect to see it in written form, except possibly as a line of dialogue in a play or in prose fiction.

A language can be said to have a neutral, standard variety if there is a way of expressing most utterances without committing oneself to forms marked as functionally limited — for instance, forms that are stylistically marked as "high" or "low," that are appropriate only for

distinctly non-standard.  Notice, though, that no difference in pronunciation is implied by the choice of, say, *thru* vs. *through*.

writing, or only for informal speech. Yet in this relatively ordinary sentence, for three of the features — the instrumental plural, the first-person plural of the conditional, and the locative singular masculine adjective — there is no such form. There are two variants in each instance, one the authors call CC and the other SC. These variants seem to be equally functionally limited in that employing a form outside its expected sphere is interpreted either as a faux pas (inadequate control of the language situation, either more generally or momentarily) or as a deliberate stylistic effect, e.g. foregrounding, or distancing oneself from a point through irony or citation.[36]

The status of the phonemic distinctions CC /ɛj/ – SC /iː/ and CC /#vo/ – SC /#o/ — both of which are found in the above example — is less clear-cut. While /ɛj/ – /iː/ is also claimed to be a distinguishing feature of CC vs. SC, there is evidence that it may not have the same functional parameters as the three morphological features given above. There is also evidence that the /#vo/ – /#o/ distinction is not as symmetric as the morphological distinctions given above, with /#o/ occupying functional space in CC while /#vo/ lacks application in SC. These matters will be examined in more detail when the data are considered in Chapter 5.

It is the lack of purely neutral morphemes, though, and the overall consistency with which we can identify these non-neutral features as "standard" or "common," that is the most solid basis for the claim that Czech has two coexisting codes, both of which are drawn upon in various ways in the discourse. In Chapter 5 we will consider the extent to which these consistent distinctions permeate Czech as it is used.

## 3.2. Historical factors interfering in descriptive work

Although the phonemic correspondences in chart 2.3.1 are the most frequently attested features distinguishing CC and SC, they are not as regular as the chart implies. The explanation for this lies in the development of Czech phonology. Old and early modern Czech had four high unrounded vowels, /i/, /ɨ/, /iː/ and /ɨː/. The vowels /ɨ/ and /ɨː/ were high central vowels; they appeared after historically unpalatalized consonants, while the front vowels /i/ and /iː/ appeared after historically palatalized consonants. These vowels were written as *i, í* (front vowels), *y, ý* (central vowels). The diphthongization to /ɛj/ affected only the long high central vowel. The long high front vowel was unaffected, as seen in chart 3.2.1.

**Chart 3.2.1. Phonemic changes in early modern Czech**

---

*ý > ej*, phonologically /ɨː/ > /ɛj/
but not *í > ej*, phonologically /iː/ > /ɛj/.

---

---

[36] The terms "foregrounding" and "backgrounding" are used here in the sense that selecting a marked code variant can bring an item to the "foreground," or the text's apparent center of current concern, where it might otherwise remain in the "background" (material assumed to be generally known or accepted by both the producer and receiver of the text).

Later in the history of Czech, the front high and central high vowels merged, the palatalization of consonants having by and large long since ceased to be a distinctive feature before high vowels.[37] In the revived standard pronunciation of the nineteenth century, written *i* and *y* were thus both pronounced [ɪ], and written *í* and *ý* were analogously pronounced as [iː], even though words containing *ý* were now consistently realized with the diphthong [ɛj] in the spoken language.

The net effect of this state of affairs is that SC /iː/ does not correspond everywhere to CC /ɛj/. In fact, there are many places where SC /iː/ corresponds to CC /iː/, and thanks to the loss of distinctive palatalization in Czech, there are no regular conditioning environments for this correspondence. The apparent predictability of SC *ý* – CC /ɛj/ is based on a sort of *trompe l'oeil*, since *ý* does not correspond to an independent phoneme in contemporary Czech.[38] It rests on our accepting SC as a purely written variety, and CC as a purely spoken one.

The correspondence SC /ɛː/ vs. CC /iː/ is problematic for different historical reasons. The sixteenth-century sources on which nineteenth-century SC is based reflect an ongoing shift in the long vowel system: the high long vowels /iː/, /uː/ were diphthongizing to /ɛj/, /ou/, while the mid long vowels /ɛː/, /oː/ were being raised to /iː/, /uː/. The nineteenth-century codifiers adopted one of these changes in full (/oː/ > /uː/), one in part (/uː/ > /ou/, but only word-internally), one occasionally (/ɛː/ > /iː/) and one not at all (the aforementioned /iː/ > /ɛj/). Recent language authorities have been even more accepting of doublets with /iː/ alongside older /ɛː/, especially when the phoneme occurs in word roots and derivational morphemes. It is the unpredictable nature of this correspondence, then, that makes it difficult to determine whether forms are to be considered SC or CC. Doublets in SC like *okénko* vs. *okýnko* 'service window', *prohlédnout* vs. *prohlídnout* 'examine', *polévka* vs. *polívka* 'soup' are corroboration that the phoneme /iː/ as a reflex of historical /ɛː/ enjoys a certain respectability in modern SC. This definitional problem is so slippery that Gammelgaard (1997:122) declines to give statistics for this correspondence in word-root environments on account of the unclear status of many such forms.

**Chart 3.2.2.  Order of phonemic changes in early modern Czech**

---

*Prothesis:*  o > vo / #_
*Diphthongization:*  uː > ou
*Raising:*  oː > uː

---

[37] "Palatalization" is retained only with dentals, and even there its status is dubious; the modern reflexes of the old Czech palatalized dentals corresponding to the unpalatalized dentals /t/, /d/, /n/ are now best described as fully palatal consonants /c/, /ɟ/, /ɲ/.

[38] Kučera 1973 presents a compelling case for allowing Czech to have four underlying phonemes, /i/, /iː/, /y/ and /yː/, but they are all realized phonetically (in his transcription) as [i], [iː], or [ej].

The SC–CC correspondences involving back vowels also pose descriptive problems. There are three shifts that interact with each other to create these correspondences, given in chart 3.2.2 in their reconstructed historical order.

In the sixteenth century, diphthongization of high long vowels was producing the shift /uː/ > /ou/ (/kuːr̝/ > /kour̝/ 'smoke'). It seems that the shift gained acceptability in medial and final positions, but was carried through less thoroughly in initial position (/uːrad/ > ?/ourad/ 'office'), at least in written texts of that period. Meanwhile, the raising of mid long vowels continued apace, yielding /oː/ > /uː/ in all medial and final positions (/doːm/ > /duːm/ 'house').[39] The nineteenth-century codifiers of Czech accepted the /uː/ > /ou/ shift, but only in medial and final positions. As a result, the modern SC–CC contrast /uː/ – /ou/ is only realized in word-initial and root-initial environments (SC /uːrad/ vs. CC /ourad/ office'); in other environments, both /uː/ and /ou/ are found in SC and CC (/kour̝/ 'smoke' vs. /kur/ 'chorus').

Once again, Czech orthography masks this problem by having two graphemes for /uː/: ú is used for the "historical" long vowel (/uːrad/ is written úřad 'office'), whereas ů is used for the new raised vowel from old /oː/ (/duːm/ is written dům 'house'). In the absence of this graphic convention, morphological criteria (position with regard to prefix, suffix and root) would be necessary to allow us to label some occurrences of /uː/ as SC and others as neutral with respect to code. For example, in the word /suːl/ 'salt' the /uː/ is root-internal and therefore neutral with respect to code; it is written sůl, and we would not expect to find a CC variant *soul. In /suːtʃtovat/ 'reckon up' the /uː/ is root-initial, following the prefix s-. This word is therefore SC in form, and is written súčtovat; we can legitimately posit a potential CC form součtovat. (Whether or not such a CC form in fact exists is a matter of how individual lexical items have developed, as seen in 3.6.)

The historical origins of these phonological changes thus reveal a considerably muddier situation than has usually been described. The persistence of phonologically-based descriptions of the SC–CC dichotomy no doubt owes much to the confluence of two trends: the attractive regularity that orthographic conventions lend to the opposition; and the tendency among linguists, who are familiar with the historical roots of the problem, to impose what is essentially a historically-justified description on a more opaque synchronic situation. It is no wonder that some Czech scholars prefer to describe the SC–CC dichotomy as morphology-based, and not phonology-based, despite the far higher occurrence of these supposedly phonologically-based correspondences (Hronek 1972:20). This relatively weak correspondence between graphic appearance and phonemic reality in the case of these vowels plays a part in my decision to downgrade the status of the phonemic oppositions in Chapter 7.

The effect of these changes can be seen in chart 3.2.3 below. The chart juxtaposes *written* standard Czech with *spoken* non-standard Czech, meaning that we consider the *graphic form* of SC items in developing our correspondences, but the *phonetic value* of CC items.

---

[39] This change would not have occurred word- and root-initially, as the shift /#o/ > /#vo/ would have removed the word- and root-initial environments for the change.

**Chart 3.2.3. Graphemes vs. phonemes**

| gloss | SC form | CC form | commentary |
|-------|---------|---------|------------|
| 'carry' | nést /nɛːst/ | nýst /niːst/ | í, ý equate to one CC phoneme: |
| 'milk' | mléko /mlɛːko/ | mlíko /mliːko/ | reflexes of /ɛː/ after a hard or ambivalent consonant |
| 'trip' | výlet /viːlɛt/ | vejlet /vɛjlɛt/ | í, ý equate to separate SC |
| 'more' | víc(e) /viːt͡s, viːt͡sɛ/ | víc /viːt͡sɛ/ | grapho-phonemes, with differing reflexes in CC. |

However, this is not to say that the SC and CC variants of morphological features given in chart 2.3.1 all have the same value and function. We can distinguish at least two major groupings: those in which the SC form is considered bookish and the CC form is now considered neutral in a variety of SC-type settings; and those in which the SC form retains wide usage in those settings and the CC form is not acceptable in the majority of them. Within these groupings there are further gradations, discussed at greater length in 3.4ff.

This situation has been brought about, paradoxically, by two closely related factors: the strong prescriptivist tradition in Czech language use, and the existence of a regulatory body for the Czech language. The introduction, conservation and prescription of archaic morphological features in the nineteenth and early twentieth centuries perpetuated the use of many features in writing and official contexts that had long since disappeared from the spoken language. With the establishment of the Czech Language Institute, the traditional purist avoidance of CC began to change, and a number of variants previously ruled non-standard were "codified" for use in the standard language, as mentioned earlier in 2.1. These rulings have primarily come in the area of morphology. Codification has continued apace in the last few decades, and while some of the earlier rulings are by now relatively uncontroversial, a few recent ones have been the subject of pointed discussion. Some examples, including those cited in 2.1, are given in chart 3.2.4 below.

In grammars and writings on Czech language culture, we find significant discrepancies of opinion as to the "proper" functions of these forms. Few look askance at CC *pracuju* 'I work' in non-formal situations alongside SC *pracuji*, but there are substantial reservations about the propriety of CC *třech* 'three (genitive plural)' as opposed to SC *tří*. Former CC infinitives like *psát* 'write' have replaced the old SC form *psáti* in virtually all contexts, to the point where the old SC ending is now extremely unusual; however, the codification of CC *píšou, pracujou* 'they write, work', with the ending -*ou* in the third-person plural non-past of verb classes 5 and 6, has not resulted in the wholesale loss of the traditional SC form, and the use of the CC form in all but the most unofficial contexts is frowned on by many (see, for example, Uličný 1995, Pálková 1994).

**Chart 3.2.4. Some SC and CC morphological variants**

| description | SC | CC |
|---|---|---|
| 1. sg. non-past in -*i* vs. -*u* following a soft consonant (feature 12) | pracuji 'I work' | pracuju 'I work' |
| genitive case of some numbers | tří 'three' | třech 'three' |
| infinitive of verbs in classes 2-6: -*ti* vs. -*t* | psáti 'to write' | psát 'to write' |
| 3. pl. non-past in -*í* vs. -*ou* in classes 5 and 6 (feature 11) | pracují 'they work' | pracujou 'they work' |
| 3. pl. non-past in -*ejí* (-*ějí*) vs. -í in class 3 (feature 16) | sázejí 'they gamble' | sází 'they gamble' |
| 3 pl. non-past in -*í* vs. -*ejí* (-*ějí*) in classes 3 and 4 (feature 13) | prosí 'they ask' | prosej(í) 'they ask' |

The situation in the third-person plural non-past of classes 3 and 4 is even more confusing. SC has traditionally maintained an idiosyncratic distribution of -*í* and -*ejí* (-*ějí*) endings for verbs whose infinitives end in -*et* (-*ět*). Most Bohemian CC has levelled the endings to a uniform -*ej(í)*/-*ěj(í)*: *prosí* > *prosej(í)*, by analogy to *sázej(í)*. However, some dialects have gone in the reverse direction, levelling all third-person plural endings to -*í*: *sázejí* > *sází*, by analogy to *prosí*. The latter variant has been codified for use in SC, while the former has not. However, the newly codified -*í* variant is noted in the PMČ as *stylově nižší* 'stylistically lower' (329), and has come under attack from Sgall as the lamentable codification of a hypercorrection, probably akin to codifying English *between you and I*.[40]

The partial codification of CC morphology for use in SC has one sense introduced a new layer of linguistic complexity into Czech. In addition to the "unrecognized" forms cited from Sgall et al. in 3.1a, there is now also a substantial class of "recognized" CC forms which have not automatically become the functional equals of the traditional SC forms. Problems like this have led linguists to investigate the usage of these morphological variants and their interaction with other sorts of variants. These studies will come under scrutiny in 3.4ff.

---

[40]  Sgall 1999:168. (The English analogy is mine, not Sgall's, although I believe it illustrates his point clearly enough.) Sgall has been a longtime proponent of the codifying of CC forms; to see him arguing against this particular codification throws into sharp relief the heterogeneous nature of these variants lumped under the label "CC."

### 3.3. Czech as an example of diglossia

As seen in 1.4, the characteristics of *diglossia* as defined in Ferguson 1959 have a strong resonance for Czech, especially in Ferguson's description of the social evaluation of the two varieties.[41] Without exhaustively rehashing evidence presented in other works: SC is a prestigious variety, with a long literary tradition; it is exclusively a taught language, not a native dialect. It constitutes, along with CC, a single phonological system, and CC grammar is in many respects a reduced form of SC.

There are, however, problems with treating contemporary Czech as a case of diglossia. One objection is that the differences between the two codes is not great enough. For Czech, the vast majority of tokens (both lexical and grammatical) are common to both SC and CC. This objection can be dealt with by appealing to later definitions of diglossia that allow the two varieties, H and L, to converge at a number of points. Paolillo 1997 offers four characterizations of diglossia that are worth recapitulating. Ferguson's original definition argued that H and L are "highly divergent varieties of the same language"; later definitions (Fishman) removed the requirement for structural relatedness of H and L, leaving behind only the existence of a community with one language functioning as H and another as L; a third view (De Silva) holds that "H and L are not distinct but are structurally related along a continuum" and a fourth (Gair) that they are "distinct in grammar only but structurally related." (Paolillo 1997:269-270). Czech would not meet Ferguson's original criteria today, but the third and fourth sorts of definitions could describe the Czech situation fairly well.

A second objection to treating Czech as a strictly diglossic situation is that if it were so, the use of varieties would be dictated exclusively by the type of discourse (situational code-switching). There is abundant evidence that code-switching in Czech is far more pervasive than that. The two most complete studies of usage — Hammer 1985 and Gammelgaard 1997 — show respectively that strings or fragments of SC occur all the time in conversation, often several times in a single sentence, and that CC forms and structures show a high degree of penetration into certain kinds of modern literature. These switches can represent *stylistic mixing* or the creation of a *deliberately formal* or *informal effect*. Sometimes they are consciously code-related, showing *irony* or promoting a certain sort of *characterization*, and sometimes they function as references to an external text, in a form of *intertextuality*.[42]

---

41   Some researchers have judged the match a perfect fit, while others have had reservations. Grygar-Rechziegel 1990 finds little to differentiate Czech from Ferguson's examples, while Micklesen 1978 goes so far as to call the Czech language situation "a classic example of diglossia as defined in all its facets by Ferguson" (437). Bílý 1999 says likewise that: "According to the criteria presented in classical sociolinguistic works, such as Ferguson 1959 or Fishman 1971, there can hardly be any doubt about the existence of Czech diglossia" (92). Sgall et al. (1992:14-18 and elsewhere) take a more reserved attitude toward the concept, noting that while Czech "displays properties characteristic of diglossia, there are also substantial differences" (17). Dickins (1995:22-23) likewise has some reservations about applying the term unreservedly to Czech.

42   Gammelgaard subsumes many of these functions under what she terms the "aesthetic function" of code-mixing. Of course, Hammer dealt exclusively with the Czech of

The speed and frequency with which the "codes" can alternate would seem to rule out diglossia as a possible description. In texts collected and analyzed by Hammer, Townsend, Short, Müllerová and others, these codes switch several times in a sentence — they can even switch over in mid-word. This fact calls into doubt even the most liberal definition of communicative code-switching, such as that proposed by Richard Hudson, which is far more permissive than earlier definitions like that of Gumperz (1972); some scholars, like Kraus, have proposed that we are witnessing not "switching" but a continuous oscillation.[43]

Ferguson's definition of diglossia does, however, point up a further difficulty: inherent in the differing traditions and intended purposes of high and low varieties is a problematic lack of parallelism. SC is a learned variety. Mastering it, or any other "high" variety, depends on the speaker's awareness of rules. The ultimate arbiter of whether an item is SC is not an educated native speaker, but a set of books, including certain dictionaries, grammars and spelling manuals published by the Czech Language Institute and other well-respected institutions. CC, on the other hand, is not defined or codified in any official manner. Its only arbiters are native speakers, preferably — but not necessarily — educated ones from certain parts of the Czech Republic. There is a danger that one can pay lip service to this disjunction, but then at certain points (notably in the lexicon and syntax, but also in phonology and morphology) implicitly accept a privative opposition model, in which anything not codified as fully acceptable for all SC contexts becomes a feature of CC.[44] Such an approach wallpapers over problems, hindering our understanding of the SC-CC dichotomy instead of improving it.

### 3.4. Empirical work on language values and language usage

Even proponents of the code-switching model acknowledge its limitations. The basic model, for instance, does not explain the substantial variations in acceptability and usage that exist between SC and CC variants. (Ideally, in fact, "CC" and "SC" would be relatively homogeneous labels for items that occurred more or less consistently in their expected contexts.) One way to increase the sophistication of the model is to create a series of gradations within each variety, or to establish other sorts of systems that intersect with the SC vs. CC system. This can be done either *empirically*, by collecting data and using it to create a model, or *inductively*, by appealing to native-speaker intuition to classify different elements.

---

educated professionals, and Gammelgaard used the writing of some of modern Czech's most skillful stylists as her material. Such mixing is undoubtedly far less common among those who read less and have less education.

[43]  Short, for instance, detects no rhyme or reason in some of the seemingly arbitrary CC-SC switches found in his study (1992:206).

[44]  Townsend 1990 skirted this pitfall in the only practical way: he used a panel of native speakers to evaluate the acceptability of various features in a series of interviews. This method has the highly desirable effect of separating those items that are merely "non-standard" from "acknowledged" CC items (Townsend's term). However, overt acceptability judgments cause their own problems, as will be shown in section 3.4.

At least six studies (or series of studies) have attempted to set up an empirical model of Czech usage, looking both at SC elements in the spoken language and at CC elements in standard discourse. All six of these research programmes (Kučera (1955, 1958, 1961, 1973); Kravčišinová and Bednářová (1968); Hammer (1985 and later articles revisiting this data); Townsend (1990, 1993); and Gammelgaard (1997)) sort the features of CC and SC into hierarchies. The hierarchies fall into two basic types: *acceptability hierarchies* and *usage hierarchies*. In the first sort of study (Kučera; Townsend 1990), native informants were asked for their judgments on forms and combinations of forms; the results were used to establish what amount to usage norms of CC and SC elements. In the second sort of study (Kravčišinová and Bednářová; Townsend 1993; Hammer; Gammelgaard) researchers attempted to quantify usage patterns in certain texts or situations and apply their conclusions to the language as a whole. By convention, they expressed their results in terms of the frequency or acceptability of the non-standard variant (CC) in certain types of discourse.

The studies each focused on a certain type or types of text. Kučera, Hammer, Townsend 1990 and Kravčišinová & Bednářová were interested in how acceptable various SC features were in educated speech and public spoken discourse. Townsend 1993 and Gammelgaard were concerned with the occurrence of non-standard features in written discourse. They concluded that CC features permeate literary discourse to differing degrees (Gammelgaard, Townsend 1993), while SC features are present in ordinary spoken discourse in varying proportions (Hammer, Kučera, Townsend 1990, Kravčišinová & Bednářová).

Particularly interesting is the finding (from Kučera's and Kravčišinová & Bednářová's work, and confirmed in later studies by Hammer and by Gammelgaard) that the frequency of CC phonemes is related to both the perceived acceptability of any particular phoneme and its position in the word. The hierarchies they established are not exactly identical, but they show striking similarities, as seen in charts 3.4.1 and 3.4.2 — which are made all the more striking by the significantly different methodologies they employed.[45]

**Chart 3.4.1. Kučera 1955**

---

*Frequency and hierarchy of CC phonemes, percentages:*

|  |  |
|---|---|
| iː (84.8; 78.2) | feature D |
| > -ɛjC/-ɛj (83.5; 70.6) | features E2, E1 |
| > -ɛj- (60.1; 36.7) | feature E3 |
| > #vo (42.9; 20.9) | feature F |
| > #ou (22.9; 7.6) | feature G |

---

[45]   Features are marked with alphanumeric labels according to a key found in appendices 2 and 3. These labels are my own; they are not found in the works concerned. I have also modified the phonetic conventions to bring them into conformity with those found elsewhere in this work.

**Chart 3.4.2. Kravčišinová and Bednářová 1968**

*Percentages for CC variants, phonemic features:*

|  |  |
|---|---|
| -ɛj (95) | feature E1 |
| > -iːC (93) | feature D2 |
| > -iː (87) | feature D1 |
| > #vo (81) | feature F |
| > -ɛjC (71) | feature E2 |
| > -ɛj- (58) | feature E3 |
| > -iː- (45) | feature D3 |
| > #ou (6) | feature G |

*Percentages for CC variants, morphological features:*

|  |  |  |
|---|---|---|
|  | velar alternations in first-person singular non-past: *můžu* (96) | feature 8 |
| > | infinitives in -*t*: *říct* (90) | feature 14 |
| > | first-person singular non-past in -*ju*: *pracuju* (89) | feature 12 |
| > | *l*-truncation in past participles: *nes* (79) | feature 9 |
| > | first-person plural conditional auxiliary: *bysme* (75) | feature 2 |
| > | levelling in neuter nominative plural adjectives: *dobrý auta* (69) | feature 3 |
| > | levelling in masculine inanimate and feminine nominative plural adjectives:  *dobrý stoly* (68) | ---46 |
| > | velar alternations in third-person plural non-past: *můžou* (57) | feature 7 |
| > | instrumental plural in -*ma*: *pánama, kostma* (53) | feature 10 |
| > | truncation in third-person plural non-past: *dělaj, sázej* (43) | feature 5 |
| > | levelling in masculine animate nominative plural adjectives:  *dobrý hráči* (39) | feature 4 |
| > | third-person plural non-past in -*jou*: *pracujou* (34) | feature 11 |
| > | first-person plural non-past truncation: *vedem* (29) | feature 17 |
| > | third-person plural non-past in -*ej(í)*: *prosej(í)* (28) | feature 13 |
| > | third-person plural non-past in -*í*: *sází* (13). | feature 16 |

Kučera employed native speakers as commentators on given texts; they were asked to rephrase spoken items as they would themselves use them (the *frequency* number given in chart 3.4.1). They were then presented with a list of forms including ones they had not chosen, and asked to evaluate their acceptability (the *hierarchy* number in chart 3.4.1).

---

46 It is unusual to see this classed as a morphological feature when data from it should also be fed into the phonological correspondences (feature D1). It therefore was not entered in my table of strictly "morphological" features.

Kravčišinová and Bednářová analyzed a series of radio programs, formal presentations and informal conversations, recording the usage of CC and SC variants in phonology and morphology. (Some of the CC elements evaluated in their study have since been accepted into SC as stylistically or functionally limited features, and these will be noted in the discussion below.)

### 3.5. Predicting usage from values

Kučera made two striking claims in his acceptability studies. First, he asserted that the acceptability frequency of CC phonemes amounted to a set of restrictions governing their combination. In this account, a CC phoneme cannot appear in a phrase unless all CC phonemes with higher acceptability ratings are realized as well. For instance, the phrases *vo tom ouřadě* /vo tom ouɽajɛ/ and *vo tom úřadě* /vo tom uːɽajɛ/ 'about that office' are both acceptable, because the CC feature /#vo/ outranks /#ou/ in acceptability (F > G). However, *\*vo mlýně* /vo mliːɲɛ/ 'about the mill' is unacceptable, because the CC feature /-ɛj-/ outranks /#vo/ in acceptability (E > F), and we would therefore expect /-ɛj-/ in place of /-iː-/. If true, this is a powerful argument for the validity of this sort of study.

Another example of this sort of restriction concerns the possibility for variation in a root and an adjectival ending in close proximity. In the example in chart 3.5.1, four possibilities exist, of which only three are realizable, according to Kučera.

**Chart 3.5.1. Kučera's possible variants for Adj-N combinations**

| gloss: 'every week' | SC variant in ending (E1) | CC variant in ending (E1) |
| --- | --- | --- |
| SC variant in root (E3) | /kaʒdiː tiːdɛn/ | /kaʒdɛj tiːdɛn/ |
| CC variant in root (E3) | */kaʒdiː tɛjdɛn/ | /kaʒdɛj tɛjdɛn/ |

Kučera's panel were given variations on the phrase *každý týden* 'every week', in which the adjective *každý* 'every' can have either a SC /iː/ ending or a CC /ɛj/ ending, and the noun *týden* 'week' can have either a SC vowel /iː/ or a CC vowel /ɛj/ in the root. According to Kučera, SC adjectival endings were rejected by his panel in combination with CC roots, meaning that all variations were possible except */kaʒdiː tɛjdɛn/. It is unclear how far these restrictions stretch; Kučera refers only to "juxtaposed morphemes or words," while noting that:

...preliminary investigations showed that the greater the distance in the sequence between morphemes in which elements characteristic of the two codes occur, the greater also the hesitation of the native informant when his reaction to the various combinations of such elements was requested (1958:185).

Kučera's second major claim was that within a single spoken word or morpheme, CC morphology can combine with SC phonology, while the reverse is not acceptable.[47] For example, the instrumental plural ending for adjectives has both a CC and SC morph, and also contains a phoneme that varies depending on the language variety. In theory there are four possibilities: a SC phoneme with SC morphology; a SC phoneme with CC morphology; a CC phoneme with SC morphology; a CC phoneme with CC morphology, as shown in chart 3.5.2.

**Chart 3.5.2. The instrumental plural adjective ending**

|                      | SC /i:/ (E2) | CC /ɛj/ (E2) |
| -------------------- | ------------ | ------------ |
| SC morph -*mi* (10)  | i:mɪ         | ɛjmɪ         |
| CC morph -*ma* (10)  | i:ma         | ɛjma         |

In actuality, Kučera says, only three of these variants are used. A form like *s takovýma lidma* 'with such people', with SC /i:/ and CC instrumental plural endings in -*ma*, is acceptable, while the form *\*s takovejmi lidmi*, with CC /ɛj/ and SC instrumental plural endings in -*mi*, would be unacceptable. This suggests that the functional distinctions between CC and SC morphological units are not the same as the distinctions between CC and SC phonological units, and that it is morphological criteria which create a CC text, not phonological ones. If true, it would be a blow against the view of CC and SC as codes defined by more or less functionally uniform variants of features.

In a later work (Kučera 1973), Kučera revised his hypothesis, finding that while his 1958 morphology-phonology hierarchy held for certain test situations, there were others where the predicted ordering was reversed (i.e. in which CC phonology combined with SC morphology but not vice versa). According to Kučera 1973, the morphology-phonology hierarchy holds in the instances set out in chart 3.5.3 below. A few remarks about his hierarchies are in order.

Two of the environments in chart 3.5.3 — numbers 2 and 3 — have SC forms which are so old-fashioned as to be archaic. The infinitive in -*i* is by now rarely used, and the verb *téct* rarely has the forms *teku, tećeš*, these having been supplanted in ordinary usage by *teču, tečeš* (PMČ 327). In both instances the first variant has largely been removed from active use in the language. This change was taking place as Kučera's twenty-year investigation into the subject was evolving. Language change, in effect, outstripped the pace of scholarly research.

We should note the acceptability of mixing varieties not only within words (environments 2-5) but also within portmanteau morphs (environment 1 and potentially 6 as well), and the fact that the morphology-phonology hierarchy is weaker in environment 5 and reversed in environment 6. These points suggest that there is substantial interpenetrability between the two varieties of Czech, and that variants are "open" in differing degrees to combining with variants from the other variety. In other words, combinability derives from the values attached to particular variants, not to morphology or phonology overall.

---

[47] This contention is strongly stated in Kučera 1958:185-186, and appears in a much milder form in Kučera 1961.

**Chart 3.5.3. Condensation of morphology-phonology hierarchies in Kučera 1973**

---

1) Instrumental plural desinence of adjectives:
   -ými /-iːmɪ/      SC phonology (iː) + SC morphology (-mɪ)
   -ejma /-ɛjma/      CC phonology (ɛj) + CC morphology (-ma)
   -ýma /-iːma/      SC phonology (iː) + CC morphology (-ma)
   *-ejmi /-ɛjmɪ/      CC phonology (ɛj) + SC morphology (-mɪ)

2) Infinitives where the SC root has a long front vowel ('be', 'bake'):
   býti, péci /biːcɪ, peːt͡sɪ/      SC phonology (iː, ɛː) + SC morphology (-cɪ, -t͡sɪ)
   bejt, píct /bɛjt, piːt͡st/      CC phonology (ɛj, iː) + CC morphology (-t, -t͡st)
   být, péct /biːt, peːt͡st/      SC phonology (iː, ɛː) + CC morphology (-t, -t͡st)
   *bejti, *píci /bɛjcɪ, *piːt͡sɪ/      CC phonology (ɛj, iː)+ SC morphology (-cɪ, -t͡sɪ)

3) Third-person plural non-past of velar-stem SC verbs in /o-/ ('they swell'):
   otekou /otɛkou/      SC phonology (#o) + SC morphology (-Kou)
   votečou /votɛt͡ʃou/      CC phonology (#vo) + SC morphology (-Čou)
   otečou /otɛt͡ʃou/      SC phonology (#o) + CC morphology (-Čou)
   *votekou /votɛkou/      CC phonology (#vo) + CC morphology (-Kou)

4) Neuter plural adjectives where the SC stem has /iː/ ('former'):
   bývalá /biːvalaː/      SC phonology (iː) + SC morphology (-aː)
   bejvalý /bɛjvaliː/      CC phonology (ɛj) + CC morphology (-iː)
   bývalý /biːvaliː/      SC phonology (iː) + CC morphology (-iː)
   ?bejvalá /bɛjvalaː/      CC phonology (ɛj) + SC morphology (-aː)

5) Third-person plural non-past of Class 6 verbs in SC /o-/ ('they liberate'):
   osvobozují /osvobozujiː/      SC phonology (#o) + SC morphology (-jiː)
   vosvobozujou /vosvobozujou/    CC phonology (#vo) + CC morphology (-jou)
   osvobozujou /osvobozujou/      SC phonology (#o) + CC morphology (-jou)
   ?vosvobozují /vosvobozujiː/      CC phonology (#vo) + SC morphology (-jiː)

6) Third-person plural non-past of Class 5 verbs with SC /ɛː/ in the stem ('they fly'):
   létají /lɛːtajiː/      SC phonology (ɛː) + SC morphology (-ajiː)
   lítaj /liːtaj/      CC phonology (iː) + CC morphology (-aj)
   ?létaj /lɛːtaj/      SC phonology (ɛː) + CC morphology (-aj)
   lítají /liːtajiː/      CC phonology (iː) + SC morphology (-ajiː)

   \* = unacceptable form; ? = questionable form

---

Kravčišinová and Bednářová, whose work addressed some of the findings in Kučera's early studies, take strong issue with Kučera's claims for a strict phonological hierarchy. Their data provide absolutely no proof of the existence of such a hierarchy; contraventions of hierarchical order are far more numerous in their study than examples following the hierarchy. As they note, Kučera's methodology open him to certain questions. His research consisted of asking native-speaker émigrés for their evaluations of the "acceptability" of set words and phrases with or without CC variants inserted. This methodology, they argue with Daneš 1957, is unreliable; the absence of this hierarchy in recorded speech shows that it is based on opinions rather than on actual usage. In a 1993 article, Kraus formulated a definition of language norms that includes both types of findings:

> Actual usage and its evaluation — even if they involve the same person — often reveal deep contradictions. For example, statistics prove convincingly that in formal situations educated persons speaking formally often use the pronunciations *degret, dizertace* 'decree, dissertation' instead of the standard *dekret, disertace*. However, these empirically observed usages are almost universally rejected as features of extremely uneducated pronunciation, even by the perpetrators themselves. One might conclude from this that a language posesses two norms: one of actual usage and one of language evaluations. (Kraus 1993:44)

Similar queries could be raised about the usage panel employed in Townsend 1990, who were asked to rate features as either "recognized" or "not recognized" for Prague CC: do the speakers' usage patterns match their value judgments? The worth of such value judgments and their bearing on the analysis of literary texts will be taken up in 5.1-5.4.

### 3.6. The inductive approach to varieties

A fundamental problem with the empirical approach is that statistics can hide the truth about usage instead of revealing it. Statistics tempt us to assume that each time we see a CC or SC feature in a written or spoken text, the speaker had a choice between two forms with roughly the same functions. For example, if we are tracking the frequency of the phonemic variants SC *ý* (/iː/) = CC *ej* (/ɛj/), we posit that all tokens of the frequently used prefix *vý-* (/viː/) are SC, while all tokens that appear as *vej-* (/vɛj/) are CC. In other words, the possible pairs *výlet–vejlet, výbor–vejbor, výčitka–vejčitka* should have the distribution in chart 3.6.1.

**Chart 3.6.1. Idealized distribution of functions for *vý-/vej-***

| SC contexts | CC contexts | functions |
|---|---|---|
| *výlet* /viːlɛt/ 'trip' | *vejlet* /vɛjlɛt/ | standard vs. non-standard |
| *výbor* /viːbor/ 'committee' | *vejbor* /vɛjbor/ | standard vs. non-standard |
| *výčitka* /viːtʃɪtka/ 'reproach' | *vejčitka* /vɛjtʃɪtka/ | standard vs. non-standard |

In fact, we find that the distribution of these forms by reported function is quite different, as shown in chart 3.6.2. While *výlet–vejlet* has the expected pattern, the doublet *výbor–vejbor* exists, but with a different distribution. In many contexts where a CC form is expected, *výbor* would nonetheless be the stylistically neutral choice, not *vejbor*. Furthermore, there is supposedly no CC context in which we will find *\*vejčitka* instead of *výčitka*.[48] Counting the latter as a token of SC in our corpus could skew the results, inasmuch as this word does not participate in the SC–CC dichotomy.

**Chart 3.6.2. Actual distribution of functions**

| SC contexts | CC contexts | functions |
|---|---|---|
| *výlet* /viːlɛt/ 'trip' | *vejlet* /vɛjlɛt/ | standard vs. non-standard |
| *výbor* /viːbor/ 'committee' | *výbor, vejbor*/viːbor, vɛjbor/ | neutral vs. emotive |
| *výčitka* /viːtʃɪtka/ 'reproach' | *výčitka* /viːtʃɪtka/ | one form for all functions |

The depressing implication of this state of affairs is that we would need to test the relationship between each CC word and its SC equivalent to make our statistics meaningful, and that studies like Kučera's are flawed by virtue of their reliance on a small set of words used to test CC features. In eliciting judgments from native speakers on set texts, Kučera introduced an unwanted variable: different morphemes show different degrees of "penetrability" with respect to CC phonemes. If the examples Kučera chose to represent /-iː-/ vs. /-ɛj-/, for instance, were highly penetrable lexemes, then the frequency and hierarchical ranking of CC forms would be much higher than for the class as a whole.

All attempts to introduce such routine testing of lexemes have so far yielded primarily *inductive* or *intuitive* classification systems, in which researchers use their own linguistic sensibility and knowledge to sort words and features into linguistic categories, instead of tallying results gleaned from non-linguists. The best example is a system first put forth by Jiří Hronek (see Hronek 1972, Sgall and Hronek 1992). For phonological and morphological features, Hronek proposed a scheme of *geographic distribution* crossed with *function*. For the lexicon, Sgall and Hronek (1992) use a different grid where each element belongs to both a 'layer' (*vrstva*) and a 'style' (*styl*), described in more detail in 5.4.

---

48  Information on the doublets *výbor–vejbor* and *výčitka–\*vejčitka* comes from Hronek 1972:21. It appears again in Sgall et al. 1992:81, where the problem of "CC phonology" is discussed in a much wider context and with more examples.

**Chart 3.6.3. Hronek's classifications (1972:19-22)**

---

**Geographical rank:**
I.   Common in conversation almost everywhere Czech is spoken.
II.  Commonly used in Bohemia and across Western Moravia, sometimes elsewhere in Moravia as well.
III. Used in Bohemia and some West Moravian towns, rarely elsewhere.
IV.  Used only in part of Bohemia (typically one or two of the three major subvarieties of Common Czech: central, eastern and southwestern speech).

**Functional rank:**
A.   CC elements that are used and accepted in SC speech contexts.
B.   Non-SC, but normal in everyday conversation, where no "standard" tone is being attempted.
C.   Non-SC, in specifically informal situations and with a certain color (familiar, crude); more universal in rural speech.

---

Čermák 1987 takes a further step in developing, on the basis of Hronek 1972, a scheme for classifying the use of forms from Common Czech and other spoken forms of the language in written texts.[49] He assigned each item a grade for frequency in the spoken code and acceptability of use in written texts; the grades are given in chart 3.6.4.

**Chart 3.6.4. Čermák's grades for CC features (1987:142)**

---

| *Frequency in spoken code* | *Acceptability in written texts* |
|---|---|
| a = always/most instances | A = accepted, used as normal |
| b = often | B = accepted sometimes |
| c = less often | C = accepted seldom or never |

---

A feature such as, for example, number 13, *prosej(í)* (i.e. the levelling of third-person plural non-past forms of certain verb classes to *-ej(í)*), gets a rating of B/a, meaning that its acceptability in writing is noticeably lower than its almost universal realization in speech

---

[49] Čermák distinguishes between Common Czech as a "code" or "system" and Spoken Czech as a "functional variety" or "realization" (1987:134, 136). It would be an oversimplification to say that the former represents a *langue* and the latter a type of *parole*, but it is not too wide of the mark. To remain consistent, I have in places used the term CC where Čermák prefers Spoken Czech; as he notes, "both terms...are sometimes used here in free variation." (1987:136).

(Čermák 1987:144). Using this scale, Čermák classified many of the phonological, morphological, lexical and syntactic features found in CC. He admitted that the categories of grades and the individual grades assigned to each feature were largely subjective and deserving of testing; nonetheless, the scale is a very convenient and relatively nonjudgmental way to approach the variations in acceptability. Čermák's scale will be measured against the results of this study, which should provide a partial test of his ratings.

A recent article by Bílý, published as this monograph was going to press, proposes another way of looking at evaluative judgments. Bílý (1999:89-90) posits five categories (I, "excessively elaborate in writing and speech"; II, "normal in writing and excessively elaborate in speech"; III, "normal in writing and speech"; IV, "normal in speech but substandard in writing"; V, "substandard in writing and speech") into which he slots different variants. In essence, Bílý's plan proposes a series of gradated categories that make use of three sharply delineated possibilities for each medium, as seen in chart 3.6.5.

**Chart 3.6.5. Bílý's classification revisited**

| *category* | *I* | *II* | *III* | *IV* | *V* |
|---|---|---|---|---|---|
| *writing* | excessively elaborate <———normal———> <———substandard———> | | | | |
| *speech* | <———excessively elaborate———> <———normal———> substandard | | | | |

Bílý does not attempt a classification of all problematic features, but rather presents a selection drawing equally on lexis, morphology, and phonology. In most instances (18 out of the 23 examples advanced) Bílý classes one of the variants as "normal in speech and writing", but in five places he finds no variant to occupy this unmarked position for both speech and writing. In four of these five, however, one variant is in category II and another is in category IV, meaning that Bílý posits a simple divergence between normal spoken Czech and normal written Czech.[50] On the face of it, this seems to subvert his own assertion that there are numerous places where no form sounds right.[51] Bílý's analysis represents a step forward in introducing an acceptability cline and the (unrealized) possibility of features lacking a universally "normal" or satisfying variant, but the particular categories he has proposed are descriptively less useful than those proposed by Čermák and others.

---

[50] The final, irreconcilable example concerns the lexemes *lejno* 'excrement', *výkal* 'feces', *fekálie* 'fecal matter' and *hovno* 'shit', where the first three fall into category I and the final lexeme into category V. Words on taboo subjects make a weak case, however.

[51] My own reading is that Bílý has been far too generous in classifying many SC forms as normal for both speech and writing, but this will be easier to see later in our analysis.

### 3.7. Reevaluating the use of data on language varieties

Two main arguments were advanced earlier against the use of statistical data. The first was that they introduce distortions by rigidly using formal criteria to label a form — and thereby a portion of text — as either SC or CC. As we saw, a form like *výčitka* 'reproach', although SC in phonemic shape, is equally CC in function. The second was that studies relying on acceptability judgments may turn out simply to represent preconceptions and thus be unrelated to ordinary usage patterns. Here we would seem to be on the point of abandoning any systematic study of the language, if formal criteria are misleading and inductive ones are unreliable. Given the arguments against the relevance of both sorts of statistical data, how can their use be justified in this study and others?

The only way out of this quandary is to place significant limits on what we expect our data to give us. Adding three significant limitations to the analysis should prove helpful.

First, we will not apply our findings in a predictive way in any particular situation. In other words, just because we know the frequency of a CC variant, it does not therefore follow that we can predict the likelihood of its appearance in any particular context, nor its function in that context, unless we first consider the options available for that particular word.

Second, a judgment as to whether a segment of text is "in" CC or SC cannot derive from the realization of a single variable (e.g. /ɛj/ vs. /iː/) within that segment. This effectively means that statistical studies do not automatically give reliable evidence for code-switching on a word-by-word basis as posited in some models. Each context has to be examined individually against the background of the forms available in that situation. Further proof of this tack will be given as the data are examined.

Third, we will not be able to draw general conclusions from any study that makes use of a very limited lexical corpus. With only two or three tokens, the deforming influence of one or another lexical item will be too great to allow us to claim very much for our conclusions.

What are the advantages, though, if any, to studying data in this way? At least two distinct purposes can be discerned.

First, while "micro" level examination shows variation in the scope and availability of variants in any given word, and can shed light on why one form appears instead of another in a situation, a "macro" picture still remains: it is equally valid to argue that it is the *overall acceptability* of a CC or SC feature variant that determines its applicability in a given context. Looking at it another way, we could argue that it is the relatively low acceptability of the /-ɛj-/ variant that causes its exclusion (or its reduction in functionality) in combination with certain lexemes, such as the aforementioned *výčitka, výbor*. We will thus collect these data anyway in the hope that, later on, the results will lead us to a more integrated explanation of the features involved in this variation.

Second, we need to realize that one possible result of our analysis will be a discrediting of traditional labels like "SC" and "CC" for individual variants. In this case, a database coded into SC and CC variants of features serves as a straw man, whose main purpose is to be knocked down to make way for a more useful model. This possibility will be considered in chapter 7, where I propose reducing the number of levels on which the SC–CC opposition functions and replacing "SC" and "CC" as labels for particular variants.

## 3.8. Colloquial Czech

Whether SC's original codifiers intended it to be used eventually in ordinary speech or not, the fact remains that SC serves as a spoken language only in highly restricted contexts, and in its current form is unlikely to expand beyond those limits. A later, more moderate school, following the works of Havránek,[52] posited the existence of a layer of speech called Colloquial Czech (*hovorová čeština*), henceforth ColC.[53] This variety of Czech was said to be a spoken version of SC, but one that avoided some of SC's more blatant archaisms, while including some CC morphology and a liberal infusion of non-SC lexical items.

There has never been any clear agreement as to which features and items are included in ColC and which are excluded from it. All current definitions of it include such morphological regularizations as first-person singular non-past *pracuju 12, můžu 8*, infinitives such as *moct, tlouct 14*, and some minor features of nominal morphology. Earlier definitions excluded regularizations of the third-person plural non-past. like *pracujou 11, můžou 7, prosejí 13*; past-tense participle truncations and analogical forms like *nes 9, říznul*; and changes in nominal and adjectival paradigms like *s těma pánama 10, dobrý auta 3*, while some later definitions include some or all of these features. There is also disagreement as to the basic status of ColC. Earlier works regarded it as a basic variety or code like CC, while in later studies, scholars began to list situations in which ColC was used, implying a more limited functional range. These hedges and limitations grew more important for the continued existence of ColC as studies of usage failed to find any evidence of widespread and systematic use of ColC on a nationwide basis. From all this it is easy to suspect that ColC was posited either as a matter of wishful thinking, or on the basis of incomplete linguistic observation and information. Many scholars, both Czech and foreign, thus doubt the existence of a discrete variety that can be called ColC, labeling it a "chimera" (Daneš, cited in Sgall 1998a:30) or a leftover bit of linguistic purism (*brusičství*, Townsend 1993).

However, a recent major study of language interaction in Moravia conducted by Davidová et al. has brought forth evidence that a kind of ColC does exist in certain tightly defined contexts in the more linguistically and dialectally heterogeneous northeastern corner of the Czech Republic. Specifically, they claim that northeast Haná and Silesian dialect speakers will tend to use ColC in conversation if there are discrepancies in the interlocutors' geographic origins (i.e. if they speak different dialects) or social standing. This tendency is especially marked in situations marked for "publicness" and "officiality".

---

[52] See Thomas 1993, 1996 and Gammelgaard 1999.

[53] Hammer (1985:13-14) states that *hovorová čeština* is not *colloquial Czech* in the sense that we usually use the word "colloquial" in English; her term *Spoken Literary Czech* is a far more accurate translation. More of a hopeful program for a language variety than a description of an existing one, the unfortunate terms *hovorová čeština* and *Colloquial Czech* have nonetheless stuck in the scholarly literature. Hammer's studies are among the few to make use of her eminently more sensible terminology, and this study will thus retain the traditional nomenclature, which at least has the advantage of being equally misleading in both languages.

Their definition of ColC is also extraordinarily broad; it encompasses virtually any speech that does not make consistent use of CC, Moravian dialect or Silesian dialect phonology, even if the phonology does tilt noticeably toward that of Moravian dialects (for instance, long vowels that shorten instead of undergoing CC raising or diphthongization). Davidová et al. seem to accept most CC and dialectal morphological variants as possible components of ColC, and they do not impose any standard as to which variants must or may not be present for speech to qualify as ColC. We could then ask whether these situations are actually best described by attaching the ColC label to them, since they seem to be more an impromptu mixing of varieties or codes with one or two common points.

We could, therefore, admit that a type of ColC probably does exist, albeit in the tightly limited circumstances and the very elastic form described by Davidová et al.[54] However, the existence of this sort of ColC in Moravia hardly poses any real challenge to the contention that Bohemian speakers (or even Czech speakers in general) do not make use of a strictly codified mixture of SC and CC as their basic mode of communication.

---

[54] As Sgall has pointed out (personal communication, 1999), the public, official nature of ColC speech acts indicated in this study calls into question whether this is functionally the same creature as the ColC Havránek and others tried to define fifty years ago. Nowadays, spontaneous and fluid mixtures of the standard with interdialects are usually subsumed under the term *běžně mluvená čeština* 'everyday spoken Czech'.

## 4. The current study

This study analyzes data from three Czech novels, thereby filling a gap in the rapidly growing literature on Czech register variation. Studies in the field examining literature have to date focused on two particular areas. The first is the linguistic dimension of CC and SC in literature, examined using so-called "underground" (i.e. banned or subversive) works of the 1950s through 1980s and their descendants. Many of these works are written predominantly in CC or contain many non-SC features throughout. The preeminent study here is Gammelgaard 1997, but Townsend 1993 and Short 1992 also tackle these questions. Literary and textual functions of register variation in plays and narrative prose also come under examination. They are addressed in the abovementioned works, as well as in shorter articles by Kolářová (1996), Komárek (1996) and Linhartová (1996), among others.

In this study, I confront a different set of issues that can be defined as follows. Narrative in the overwhelming majority of Czech fiction appearing in the Czech Republic falls clearly within the boundaries of SC, thus continuing older, established traditions. Prose works whose narratives lean heavily on non-SC varieties (like Svoboda's *Autostopem kolem světa* 'Hitchhiking Around The World', Topol's *Sestra* 'Sister', etc.) are exceptions, rather than the rule. Still, no author can escape the creeping acceptability of CC, especially when portraying direct dialogue. In direct dialogue, some level of CC penetration is usual and acceptable — although, apparently, complete and consistent use of all CC features is neither usual nor acceptable. What, then, can we say about the occurrence of so-called "CC variants" in direct dialogue within these predominantly SC texts, and does it correspond to other observed feature hierarchies for SC and CC? What information, furthermore, do these hierarchies give us about the SC–CC opposition? And, since literary characters, by definition, "speak" on a "public" stage — a classic environment for ColC — is there any support for the existence of ColC in literary dialogue?

It will be clear from the above that this study focuses on the nature of written Czech, and the extent to which it can (or must) incorporate both features of SC and CC. The "dialogue" contained in the study's three novels does attempt to resemble plausible speech patterns, but it fundamentally is not, and cannot be treated as a faithful representation of spoken Czech. Transcriptions of dialogic texts like those in Müllerová et al. 1992 make it clear from the very first that ordinary speech has an entirely different structure and profile. This fact will become evident when we turn to identifying syntactic features "characteristic" of CC and SC.

### 4.1. Works in the corpus

I looked at dialogue from between 100 and 200 pages of text from each of three recent novels by Czech authors set in Prague: Ivan Klíma's *Čekání na tmu, čekání na světlo* 'Waiting for Darkness, Waiting for Light'; Pavel Kohout's *Sněžím* 'I Am Snowing'; and Lenka Procházková's *Oční kapky* 'Eye Drops'. The authors are all over 45; all were active in literary circles before the 1989 revolution, and suffered an extended period of disfavor with the Communist regime. Common to all the authors is an interest in contemporary social problems and the way they reflect the political landscape of pre- and postrevolutionary

Prague. The focus on Prague limits the linguistic scope of inquiry to the variety of Czech commonly spoken in central Bohemia.

Klíma's novel tackles the adjustment of a moderately successful, morally pliable Communist-era filmmaker to postrevolutionary existence; its style is spare and emotionally subdued. In it, the protagonist comes slowly to grips with a series of failed love affairs and with his own continuing capitulation to society's prevailing whims. Kohout's *Sněžím* is a psychological drama about the elusive nature of truth and identity after 1989, and the narrative is more emotional and expressive. Its protagonist is a woman nearing forty, whose lovers have accused each other of moral turpitude under the former regime. Set against the background of the "lustration" campaign of the early 1990s, it is told as a "whodunit," with the narrator undertaking to discover the reality behind the allegations. In *Oční kapky*, Procházková tells the story of an ill-fated love affair between a man and woman in their twenties; set in the "normalization" era of the late 1970s, her tone varies from wry to maudlin as she follows their relationship from its early days to the man's great act of betrayal and its consequences. All three novels are told largely from the viewpoint of a single main character, with Kohout working in the first person, Klíma exclusively in the third person, and Procházková switching halfway through the book from third to first person. All three novels have a further group of significant characters (two to five in number) whose speech features prominently in direct dialogue. The narration in these novels conforms precisely to what we would call SC, with occasional non-SC lexical items.

Following a preliminary study of usage,[55] I expanded the corpus, setting the size at approximately 10,000 words per novel.[56] The increased size of the corpus allowed for comprehensive coverage of all important phonological features said to mark the CC–SC divide, as well as many morphological ones. It also gave ample evidence of CC and SC lexical items and some coverage of CC and SC syntax.

### 4.2. Coding and analysis of the corpus

The corpus was coded and analyzed using BBEdit Lite 3.5.1, a freeware program intended primarily for computer code writing. It is less helpful at compiling data than a concordance

---

[55] Bermel 1997 examined a smaller corpus from each novel (appx. 5100 words from Klíma, 5300 from Kohout, and 8300 from Procházková). The data offered therein differ in detail from those of this study, but not in the overall conclusions that they suggest.

[56] Only direct speech — that found within quotation marks or equivalent punctuation — was used. In culling the dialogue from the novels, I eliminated speeches I thought might skew the data. In Kohout's novel, this included two lengthy monologues by a Slovak whose speeches appear in Czech (although it is not clear whether she is speaking Czech or whether the narrator/protagonist is providing a translation). From Klíma's work, I skipped the scenes in which the protagonist sketches a film scenario, complete with dialogue; I did not want to consider the ramifications of trying to convey a written film script in a novel. I did, however, include the few lines of public speech in Klíma's novel, as well as the occasion when the protagonist recounts to his girlfriend — complete with her interruptions — the plot of a film he hopes to make.

program is, but it has powerful search functions that allow for maximum retrieval of related items with only minimal coding; its search capabilities are particularly helpful for languages like Czech, where one feature may be realized with several possible spellings or endings. Sixty-five items were tracked using two-digit codes. These included: phonemic features in various positions; morphological features; lexical strata; and syntactic features such as subject reduplication and analytic structures. Not all coded items produced enough data for use in this study; some less frequent features may have to await the days of hassle-free text scanning and coding before it is possible to compile large enough coded databases to gather data on them.

Where possible, tokens were coded immediately before the feature searched for. For example, when coding the SC forms *mléko* 'milk' or *nést* 'to carry' the number *13* was placed before the *é*, indicating an instance of "SC /ɛ:/ = CC /i:/" in root position. In the database, the forms therefore appear as *ml13éko, n13ést*. Forms with the CC variant of item 13, however, spell /i:/ with either *í* or *ý* in the texts (typically using *ý* only in places where *í* would imply palatalization of the preceding consonant). To retrieve all words that have either an *í* or *ý* under feature 13, we search either for strings with *13* followed by *í* or *ý*, or for strings with *13* followed by any character except *é*. These methods will return both *ml13íko* and *n13ýst*. The GREP searching feature of BBEdit Lite 3.5.1 makes these alternate and excluding searches relatively painless. A list of coded features appears in appendix 4.

### 4.3. Authorship and the publication process

We also need to address the issue of editorial influence on literary dialogue. When we look at dialogue in a novel, are we in fact seeing the product of one person's work, or of numerous unseen editorial pens? Furthermore, does it matter?

To the first question: in my capacity as a reviewer and translator, I was fortunate to see pre-publication drafts of two of the novels. Virtually no changes in the dialogue had been made between draft and publication. As a result, I feel relatively confident that the dialogue in these novels is the result of the authors' own editing process, and has not been made to conform to any publishing house "style guide" in its use of SC and CC variants.

To the second question: it is not particularly relevant how many people contributed to the precise wordings and forms that appear in the novels. All of the authors used are prominent members of the Czech literary scene, and presumably have enough clout to resist intrusive stylistic impositions on the part of publishing houses. So long as the resulting published texts reflect their authors' intentions, the point is a moot one. As mentioned before, revisability is one of the characteristics of the written medium, and literary texts are by definition the end product of a lengthy creative process.

## 5. Analysis by feature type

In this chapter, I will address the extent to which it is meaningful to speak of four different "levels" on which the SC–CC opposition is realized — phonology, morphology, syntax and the lexicon. In sections 5.1 through 5.4, I will consider each of the proposed levels in turn, comparing my data to previously collected data and interpretations thereof.

One important initial question is: what proportion of these texts is composed of distinctive SC and CC features? The example quoted from Sgall et al. in 3.1a shows a sentence in which every other word has some specifically SC or CC marker. But most tokens in these texts contain no overt markers at all. Three separate thousand-word samples from the texts showed low frequencies of overt phonological, morphological and lexical code markers, as seen in chart 5.0.1. (Syntactic code markers are difficult to count reliably, as discussed in 5.4.)

**Chart 5.0.1. Marked tokens in thousand-word samples**

|  | *Procházková* | *Kohout* | *Klíma* |
|---|---|---|---|
| *CC features* | 98 | 113 | 33 |
| *SC features* | 40 | 54 | 83 |
| *Total marked features* | 138 | 167 | 116 |

The evidence from chart 5.0.1 suggests that much of these texts is composed of tokens not associated typically or exclusively with SC or CC, or any other code, for that matter. Given this relatively low occurrence, the fact that clusters of features are encountered (see 7.3) means that, conversely, there will also be stretches of text without any reliable code indicators at all. The examination of CC and SC features has to be set against this background of generally undifferentiated text, whose lexicon, phonology and morphology are common to many varieties of written Czech.

### 5.1. Phonemic features

The four phonemic markers distinguishing CC from SC are considered to be: /ɛj/ vs. /iː/ (written *ej* vs. *ý*); /iː/ vs. /ɛː/ (written *í* or *ý* vs. *é*); /vo/ vs. /o/; /ou/ vs. /uː/ (written *ou* vs. *ú*). The last two oppositions are only realized in word-initial or root-initial position, while the first two oppositions can be realized in at least three positions in the word. Previous research (Kučera; Kravčišinová and Bednářová; Hammer; Gammelgaard) identified differences in frequency and acceptability that depend on the morphological position of the phoneme in question. These works consider up to three positions: root-internal or root-final (*mlík-o* vs.

*mlék-o* 'milk'; *vej-let* vs. *vý-let* 'trip'); non-final desinence (*velk-ejch* vs. *velk-ých* 'large (masculine/neuter genitive plural)'); and desinence-final (*velk-ej* vs. *velk-ý* 'large (masculine nominative singular)').[57] I followed this breakdown in my data collection in order to facilitate comparisons. The occurrence of CC variants is given in chart 5.1.1.

**Chart 5.1.1. CC phonemic variants in literary dialogue, by frequency**

| | | |
|---|---|---|
| **Klíma:** | /iː/ for /ɛː/ in **roots** (mlíko) 11.8% | D3 |
| | > /iː/ for /ɛː/ **desinence-final** (velký auto) 6.1% | D1 |
| | > /iː/ for /ɛː/ **non-final desinence** (velkýho) 4.6% | D2 |
| | > /ɛj/ for /iː/ in **roots** (mlejn) 3.0% | E3 |
| | > others (0%) | |
| **Kohout:** | /ɛj/ for /iː/ **desinence-final** (velkej) 40.2% | E1 |
| | = /iː/ for /ɛː/ in **roots** (mlíko) 38.5% | D3 |
| | = /iː/ for /ɛː/ **desinence-final** (velký auto) 36.7% | D1 |
| | = /iː/ for /ɛː/ **non-final desinence** (velkýho) 36.4% | D2 |
| | > /ɛj/ for /iː/ in **roots** (mlejn) 26.3% | E3 |
| | > /vo/ for /o/ at **root-root boundary** (modrovokej) 16.7*% | F2 |
| | > /vo/ for /o/ **word-initially** (vodejdu) 13.6% | F1 |
| | > /ɛj/ for /iː/ **non-final desinence** (velkejch) 6.3% | E2 |
| | > /ou/ for /uː/ **word-initially** (ouřad) 0.0% | G |
| **Procházková:** | /iː/ for /ɛː/ **non-final desinence** (velkýho) 86.1% | D2 |
| | > /iː/ for /ɛː/ **desinence-final** (velký auto) 73.9% | D1 |
| | > /ɛj/ for /iː/ **non-final desinence** (velkejch) 68.4% | E2 |
| | = /ɛj/ for /iː/ **desinence-final** (velkej) 67.8% | E1 |
| | > /iː/ for /ɛː/ in **roots** (mlíko) 58.3% | D3 |
| | > /ɛj/ for /iː/ in **roots** (mlejn) 45.8% | E3 |
| | > ou/ for /uː/ **word-initial** (ouřad) 5.3% | G |
| | > /vo/ for /o/ **word-initial** (vodejdu) 0.0% | F1 |
| | = /vo/ for /o/ at **root-root boundary** (modrovokej) 0.0*% | F2 |

\* = *feature attested in less than 10 tokens*

Chart 5.1.1 shows substantial discrepancies in the frequency of CC forms between the novelists. The distribution of individual features by word position is given in chart 5.1.2.

---

[57] The only prefix that seems to participate in these contrasts is SC /viː/–CC /vɛj/. Previous researchers have treated this as a root-internal occurrence; I have done the same.

**Chart 5.1.2.  CC phonemic variants, by type and frequency**

---

| | | |
|---|---|---|
| **Klíma:** | /iː/ for /ɛː/ in **roots** (mlíko) 11.8% | D3 |
| | > /iː/ for /ɛː/ **desinence-final** (velký auto) 6.1% | D1 |
| | > /iː/ for /ɛː/ **non-final desinence** (velkýho) 4.6% | D2 |
| | | |
| | /ɛj/ for /iː/ in **roots** (mlejn) 3.0% | E3 |
| | | |
| | others (0%) | |
| **Kohout:** | /iː/ for /ɛː/ in **roots** (mlíko) 38.5% | D3 |
| | = /iː/ for /ɛː/ **desinence-final** (velký auto) 36.7% | D1 |
| | = /iː/ for /ɛː/ **non-final desinence** (velkýho) 36.4% | D2 |
| | | |
| | /ɛj/ for /iː/ **desinence-final** (velkej) 40.2% | E1 |
| | > /ɛj/ for /iː/ in **roots** (mlejn) 26.3% | E3 |
| | > /ɛj/ for /iː/ **non-final desinence** (velkejch) 6.3% | E2 |
| | | |
| | /vo/ for /o/ at **root-root boundary** (modrovokej) 16.7% | F2 |
| | > /vo/ for /o/ **word-initial** (vodejdu) 13.6% | F1 |
| | | |
| | /ou/ for /uː/ **word-initial** (ouřad) 0% | G |
| **Procházková:** | /iː/ for /ɛː/ **non-final desinence** (velkýho) 86.1% | D2 |
| | > /iː/ for /ɛː/ **desinence-final** (velký auto) 73.9% | D1 |
| | > /iː/ for /ɛː/ in **roots** (mlíko) 58.3% | D3 |
| | | |
| | /ɛj/ for /iː/ **non-final desinence** (velkejch) 68.4% | E2 |
| | = /ɛj/ for /iː/ **desinence-final** (velkej) 67.8% | E1 |
| | > /ɛj/ for /iː/ in **roots** (mlejn) 45.8% | E3 |
| | | |
| | /vo/ for /o/ **word-initial** (vodejdu) 0.0% | F1 |
| | = /vo/ for /o/ at **root-root boundary** (modrovokej) 0.0% | F2 |
| | | |
| | /ou/ for /uː/ **word-initial** (ouřad) 5.3% | G |

---

The information in chart 5.1.2 can also be conveyed in tabular form.  Chart 5.1.3 below allows us to compare all three works and their distribution of CC features at a glance.

**Chart 5.1.3. Tabular format for data from 5.1.2**

| % | D /iː/ for /eː/ | E /ɛj/ for /iː/ | F /vo/ for /o/ | G /ou/ for /uː/ |
|---|---|---|---|---|
| 100% | | | | |
| 90-99% | | | | |
| 80-89% | Pr 86.1 D2 | | | |
| 70-79% | Pr 73.9 D1 | | | |
| 60-69% | | Pr 68.4 E2 | | |
| | | Pr 67.8 E1 | | |
| 50-59% | Pr 58.3 D3 | | | |
| 40-49% | | Pr 45.8 E3 | | |
| | | Ko 40.2 E1 | | |
| 30-39% | Ko 38.5 D3 | | | |
| | Ko 36.7 D1 | | | |
| | Ko 36.4 D2 | | | |
| 20-29% | | Ko 26.3 E3 | | |
| 10-19% | Kl 11.8 D3 | | Ko 16.7 F2 | |
| | | | Ko 13.6 F1 | |
| 1-9% | Kl 6.1 D1 | Ko 6.3 E2 | | Pr 5.3 G |
| | Kl 4.6 D2 | Kl 3.0 E3 | | |
| 0% | | Kl 0.0 E1, E2 | Pr 0.0 F1, F2 | Ko 0.0 G |
| | | | Kl 0.0 F1, F2 | Kl 0.0 G |

*D1 and E1 = word-final; D2 and E2 =non-final desinence; D3 and E3 = word root*
*F1 = word-initial; F2 = root/stem initial but word-internal*
*Pr = Procházková; Ko = Kohout; Kl = Klíma*

Chart 5.1.3 yields two interesting conclusions:

1) *Hierarchies of CC phonemic variants.* The CC phoneme /iː/ is clearly the most commonly employed, with every author making use of it to some degree, in frequencies from five to 85 percent. The next in order of frequency, /ɛj/, has a range of zero to almost 70 percent. The third feature, /#vo/, occurs in only one text, in approximately 1 of every 6 contexts. The least frequent, /#ou/, occurs in approximately 1 of 20 contexts in only one text.

This hierarchy tallies closely with that of Kučera, and diverges substantially from that of Kravičišinová and Bednářová (see 3.4 above). This result is not entirely unexpected. Kučera's study was one of value judgments offered by informants on various sentences; Kravčišinová and Bednářová's study was of language as it is actually used in speech. Literary creation offers more scope for reflection and expression of values, as per Kučera's study. My data do not uphold Kučera's conclusions as universally valid for the SC–CC opposition, but they do confirm that *carefully crafted* texts conform to the sort of value judgments Kučera elicited in his survey, even when they do not set out explicitly to make such judgments. They also point out that literary texts do not necessarily reproduce the hierarchies of usage found in speech, even when they are meant to be taken as representations of speech.[58]  To use the terms proposed in Kraus 1993 (see 3.5 above), literary dialogue is best seen as a reflection of norms of evaluation rather than of norms of production.

2) *Absolute frequency of CC phonological items by text.*  The general agreement in a hierarchy of features disguises the fact that the absolute frequency of CC items differs radically from text to text.  If we ignore the single occurrence of root-internal /ɛj/, Klíma uses only one CC phoneme, /iː/, and never at a frequency above 10%, while Procházková makes use of a range of CC features, all at higher frequencies than Klíma.  In between is Kohout, who uses CC features in roughly six to 40 percent of possible contexts.  While Kučera's value hierarchy is respected, the absolute frequency of CC items can be quite high, as in Kučera's original findings, or substantially lower, with all frequencies below 15 percent.

It was mentioned earlier that certain other phonetic differences between SC and non-SC speech are often cited in the scholarly literature.  Simpler consonant clusters, the shortening of some vowels and the lengthening of others are all occasional features of spoken Czech and are sometimes labelled "CC".  Only one text (Kohout) made any sustained use of these features.  The corpora for Procházková and Klíma show only two examples in the former (*dycky* and *vem* for *vždycky* 'always' and *vezmi* 'take (imperative)') and none in the latter.  Kohout, on the other hand, has 87 examples of such forms, although their distribution is largely confined to secondary characters.  (See 6.3 for a discussion of the particular forms and their usage.)

Why are these variants virtually absent from two texts, appearing only occasionally in the third?  Gammelgaard (1997:77-83) notes that written texts balance phoneticity against intelligibility.  A text that deviates too drastically from the familiar SC orthography is difficult to process, slows down reading and risks irritating the reader.  This is the background against which all such deviations from SC occur.  Authors thus have to weigh their reasons for indicating such a pronunciation explicitly against the known drawbacks of doing so.  We might thus hypothesize that these authors in general find that the disadvantages of phonetic renderings outweigh the advantages.  Why should this be so for vowel length and consonant clusters but not for the phonemic differences discussed earlier in this section?

One explanation is that the degree of difference between these SC and non-SC variants is open to dispute.  For example, vowel length is in its realization subjective and non-binary; in speech there exist at least [nɛ], [nɛˑ], [nɛː] as realizations of *ne* 'no', and [mo̞ɾɛ], [mo̞ˑɾɛ], [mo̞ːɾɛ] as realizations of *moře* 'loads'.  With elided pronunciation, it is possible to imagine intermediate reductions of the segments (e.g. [ɲɛjak], [ɲɛak], [ɲᵉaːk] [ɲaːk] as realizations of *nějak* 'somehow', or [vʒdɪt͡skɪ], [ᵛʒdɪt͡skɪ], [ᶟdɪt͡skɪ], [dɪt͡skɪ] as realizations of *vždycky* 'always').  Pronunciation is thus not always reflected adequately by spelling.  An author might be reluctant to use a short vowel where what is desired is something between a long and a short vowel, or some intermediate degree of elision of consonants.  In these circumstances, the conventional SC spelling may stand for all possible pronunciations.

---

[58]  This discrepancy offers one explanation as to why Kučera and Gammelgaard found strict hierarchies of usage, while Kravčišinová and Bednářová found no basis for these hierarchies.  Gammelgaard, who worked on poetry and fiction, would have been dealing with conscious or unconscious aesthetic judgments on the part of her authors, bringing her study closer to Kučera's and the current study in its tenor.

Additionally, there is the stigmatized nature of these pronunciations — often cited as careless or slovenly use of language — and their aesthetic rejection by people who may in fact use them (Kraus et al. 1982, cited at length above). Townsend 1990:40, 43-45 also declines to accept these variants as normal for Prague CC on various grounds, foremost the reluctance of his consultants to do so.[59]

All these factors could potentially contribute to keeping such forms out of these texts. The virtual absence of these forms seems to confirm our hypothesis that they have a very low prestige value in written form and that it is this aesthetic judgment, rather than any indication of actual pronunciation, that prevails.

## 5.2. Morphological features

The differences between CC and SC morphology are said to be substantial. Pairs of features are established for the non-past tense forms of the verb, the past tense forms, several noun and adjective case forms, infinitives, and even adverbs. These corresponding pairs represent the work of two forces in language: analogy and reduction of output effort.

1) *Analogy.* Often the CC form is an innovation, modelled on a different declension or conjugation type, or even on an entirely different case, as seen in chart 5.2.1.

**Chart 5.2.1. Source of CC forms**

| gloss | SC form | CC form | possible model for CC form |
|---|---|---|---|
| 'I work' | pracuj-i | pracuj-u | nes-u 'I carry' |
| 'to say' | říc-i | říc-t | děla-t 'to do' |
| 'they ask' | pros-í | pros-ej(í) | přinášejí 'they bring' |
| 'with men (pl.)' | s pán-y | s pán-ama | s pán-ama 'with (both) men' (old dual) |

In all instances in chart 5.2.1, the SC form is the historically "original" form.[60]

2) *Reduction of output effort.* This is a well-known phenomenon that distinguishes all spoken languages from their written counterparts. The CC form may be a truncated or allegro (i.e. quickly or carelessly spoken) version of the SC model, or may simply be the shorter of

---

[59] Among his other reasons are the difficulty of being sure in rapid speech how long a vowel is, and the universal nature of cluster simplifications in spontaneous spoken language.

[60] Chart 5.2.1 is not meant to suggest that the specific SC "possible models" are known to be the sources for the CC forms. Rather, it suggests that *such a form* of that class or type, or even the aggregate effect of the existence of many forms of that class or type, provided the model for analogical change. (Hyphens were added to aid comparison.)

two variants inherited from Proto-Slavic, the longer of which is found in SC. Examples of reductions are SC *s dobrým* > CC *s dobrym* 'with good'; SC *dělají* > CC *dělaj* 'they do'; examples of shorter vs. longer inherited alternatives include SC *nesl* vs. CC *nes* 'he carried'; SC *vedeme* vs. CC *vedem* 'we lead'. We do not class any of these shortenings as phonemic because in modern Czech they only occur predictably in certain morphological environments.

The frequency of CC forms in these texts is set out in charts 5.2.2 and 5.2.3 (for a fuller explanation of all the features involved see chart 2.3.1). Chart 5.2.2 gives the frequency for each text; chart 5.2.3 juxtaposes the frequencies of items in all three texts.

The most clearly observable distinction is between those CC forms which have been accepted as doublets alongside SC forms and those which have not. It is certainly not surprising that for feature 14 we find the infinitives *říct, moct* 'to be able, to say' etc. instead of *říci, moci*; after all, the most recent academic grammar of Czech (Masaryk University's PMČ) lists these verbs under the *-t* form, and only deep in the explanation does it acknowledge that the *-i* form is found in older and high-style prose. Other forms acknowledged by current language standards are the first-person singular. non-past forms in *-u* vs. the older *-i* form in feature 12. Here there is less agreement as to their universal suitability. The first-person singular *-u* form is widely accepted as a "colloquial variant" but competes with the *-i* form nonetheless.[61] The third-person plural non-past *-ou* form of feature 11 seems to be less widely accepted. Usage in these texts broadly respects these value judgments, and the "acknowledged" CC forms rate at or near 100 percent in all texts, with the notable exception of third-person plural non-past *-ou* for feature 11.

With the notable exception of the first-person plural non-past form *vedem* for feature 17, "reduced-effort" features are not frequently used in these texts. These features are not accepted in SC and their frequency in texts is low. It may be that morphological truncations are perceived by authors as phonemic truncations or phonetic simplifications, so their inclusion or exclusion can simply mark tempo and carefulness of enunciation.

The absolute frequency of these features differs substantially in the novels analyzed from that offered by Gammelgaard and by Kravčišinová & Bednářová.[62] Curiously, novelistic dialogue seems to promote certain features above their occurrence in speech and demote others, as seen in chart 5.2.4 below.

---

61  The authors of the PMČ explain their use of the term *hovorové* 'colloquial' as follows: "V kultivovaných mluvených projevech najdeme taky prostředky **hovorové**. Hovorové tvary, výrazy i vetné konstrukce se z mluvené komunikace postupně dostávají i do psaných textů, především publicistických." (18) Translation: "We also find **colloquial** forms in cultivated spoken utterances. Colloquial forms, expressions and sentence structures are gradually finding their way from spoken communication into written texts as well, especially journalistic ones." (Emphasis original.) The grammar itself is aimed at "těm, kdo chtějí nebo jsou nuceni vyjadřovat se kultivovaně" ('those who want or are required to express themselves in a cultivated manner').

62  Hammer 1985 is not included here, because although she states that morphological items were counted and analyzed, she does not cite either raw numbers or statistics.

**Chart 5.2.2. CC verbal morphology in dialogue of SC texts**

---

*Klíma:*
#můžu 8 (100.0) = #říct 14 (100.0*) = #pracuju 12 (100.0) = #můžou 7 (100.0*)
> lidi 6 (77.3)
> pánama/kostma 10 (32.0)
> #pracujou 11 (28.0)
> nes 9 (20.7)
> dobrý auta 3 (14.3)
> dělaj/sázej 5 (0.0) = dobrý hráči 4 (0.0) = vedem 17 (0.0) = prosej(í) 13 (0.0)
  = bysme 2 (0.0) = #sází 16 (0.0) = bysem 1 (0.0) = s dobrym 15 (0.0*).

*Kohout:*
lidi 6 (100.0*) = #říct 14 (100.0) = #můžou 7 (100.0*)
> #pracuju 12 (92.9)
> vedem 17 (88.9)
> #pracujou 11 (75.0*)
> dobrý auta 3 (66.7*)
> dobrý hráči 4 (60.0)
> #můžu 8 (58.3)
> pánama/kostma 10 (44.0)
> nes 9 (39.0)
> prosej(í) 13 (26.7)
> s dobrym 15 (10.0)
> dělaj/sázej 5 (5.3)
> bysem 1 (3.0)
> bysme 2 (0.0*) = #sází 16 (0.0*)

*Procházková:*
#můžu 8 (100.0) = #říct 14 (100.0) = #pracuju 12 (100.0) = dobrý auta 3 (100.0*)
  = #můžou 7 (100.0*) = lidi 6 (100.0*)
> vedem 17 (78.9)
> prosej(í) 13 (71.4*)
> pánama/kostma 10 (61.1) = dělaj/sázej 5 (60.0)
> #pracujou 11 (40.0*)
> nes 9 (33.3) = dobrý hráči 4 (33.3*)
> #sází 16 (0.0*) = s dobrym 15 (0.0*) = bysme 2 (0.0) = bysem 1 (0.0)

\* = *under 10 tokens are attested*
# = *now accepted in some SC as well*

---

From charts 5.2.1-5.2.3, we can discern four distinct trends that come from comparing dialogue in the corpus with studies of authentic speech (see chart 5.2.4 below).

**Chart 5.2.3.  Tabular form of chart 5.2.2**

| % | analogy | reduced effort |
|---|---------|----------------|
| 100% | Kl #můžu 8, #říct 14*, #pracuju 12, #můžou 7* <br> Ko lidi 6*, #říct 14, #můžou 7* <br> Pr můžu 8, #říct 14, #pracuju 12, dobrý auta 3*, #můžou 7*, lidi 6* | |
| 90-99% | Ko #pracuju 12 (92.9) | |
| 80-89% | | Ko vedem 17 (88.9) |
| 70-79% | Kl lidi 6 (77.3) <br> Ko #pracujou 11 (75.0*) <br> Pr prosej(í) 13 (71.4*) | Pr vedem 17 (78.9) |
| 60-69% | Ko dobrý auta 3 (66.7*) <br> Pr pánama (61.1) <br> Ko dobrý hráči 4 (60.0) | Pr dělaj, sázej 5 (60.0) |
| 50-59% | Ko #můžu 8 (58.3) | |
| 40-49% | Ko pánama (44.0) <br> Pr #pracujou 11 (40.0*) | |
| 30-39% | Pr dobrý hráči 4 (33.3*) <br> Kl pánama (32.0) | Ko nes 9 (39.0) <br> Pr nes 9 (33.3) |
| 20-29% | Kl #pracujou 11 (28.0) <br> Ko prosej(í) 13 (26.7) | Kl nes 9 (20.7) |
| 10-19% | Kl dobrý auta 3 (14.3) | Ko s dobrym 15 (10.0) |
| 1-9% | Ko bysem 1 (3.0) | Ko dělaj/sázej 5 (5.3) |
| 0% | Kl dobrý hráči 4, prosej(í) 13, bysme 2, #sází 16, bysem 1 <br> Ko bysme 2*, #sází 16* <br> Pr #sází 16*, bysme 2, bysem 1 | Kl dělaj/sázej 5, vedem 17, s dobrym 15* <br> Pr s dobrym 15* |

*\* = less than ten tokens overall; # = now accepted in some SC as well*
*Pr = Procházková; Ko = Kohout; Kl = Klíma*

1) *Exclusive use of CC forms.*  Dialogue in literary works consistently uses some CC variants where educated and public speech is slightly more tolerant of CC–SC variation. These examples (*můžu 8, říct 14, lidi 6, pracuju 12, můžou 7*) are near the top of the table.

2) *Promotion of CC forms.*  Literary dialogue can promote certain features that are less frequent in educated and public speech.  No one feature is promoted in this way in all three works.  Two features (*vedem 17, pracujou 11*) are more prominent in Kohout and Procházková, but less prominent in Klíma, the most conservative author.  Three features (*prosej(í) 13, dělaj/sázej 5, pánama 10*) are more prominent in Procházková alone, while one (*dobrý hráči 4*) is more prominent in Kohout alone.

**Chart 5.2.4. Frequency of CC forms in written dialogue and speech**

| Feature | This study (Pr, Ko, Kl) | Kravčišinová & Bednářová | Gammelgaard (Hr, Pl)[63] |
|---|---|---|---|
| #můžu 8 | 100.0, 58.3, 100.0 | 96 | 100*, 100* |
| #říct 14 | 100.0, 100.0, 100.0 | 90 | 100*, 100* |
| lidi 6 | 100.0*, 100.0*, 77.3 | -- | 59, 75* |
| #pracuju 12 | 100.0, 92.9, 100.0 | 89 | 83*, 65 |
| nes 9 | 33.3, 39.0, 20.7 | 79 | 4, 83 |
| bysme 2 | 0.0, 0.0, 0.0 | 75 | 75*, 60* |
| dobrý auta 3 | 100.0*, 66.7*, 14.3 | 69 | 20*, 33* |
| #můžou 7 | 100.0*, 100.0*, 100.0*; | 57 | 0, 67* |
| pánama 10 | 61.1, 44.0, 32.0 | 53 | 79, 100* |
| dobrý hráči 4 | 33.3*, 60.0, 0.0 | 39 | -- |
| dělaj, sázej 5 | 60.0, 5.3, 0.0 | 43 | 0, 92 |
| #pracujou 11 | 40.0*, 75.0*, 28.0 | 34 | 75*, 80* |
| vedem 17 | 78.9, 88.9, 0.0 | 29 | 0, 30 |
| prosej(í) 13 | 71.4*, 26.7, 0.0 | 28 | 46, 100* |
| #sází 16 | 0.0, 0.0, 0.0 | 13 | -- |
| s dobrym 15 | 0.0, 10.0, 0.0* | -- | -- |
| bysem 1 | 0.0, 3.0, 0.0 | -- | -- |

3) *Demotion of CC forms.* The best example of a frequent CC feature that is demoted is *nes 9*, whose frequency in literary dialogue never reaches half its frequency in speech.[64] Klíma often demotes CC forms (*pracujou 11, pánama/kostma 10, dobrý auta 3*) below their speech frequency, as does Kohout (*můžu 8, dobrý auta 3, pánama/kostma 10*); Procházková only does so in one instance (*dobrý hráči 4*), which is relatively poorly attested.

4) *Suppression of non-SC or marginally SC forms.* Some non-SC forms are suppressed entirely in literary dialogue. Especially notable is the frequency of *bysme 2* in speech — 75 percent — versus its complete absence in literary dialogue. Many of the less-used or more stigmatized forms fall into this category, regardless of whether or not they are accepted marginally for SC, e.g. *sází* for feature 16, *s dobrym* for feature 15, *bysem* for feature 1; their occurrence in Kohout is partially anomalous, since they are found only in the speech of a character marked by strict adherence to the lowest possible CC norms. The suppression of

---

63 These figures include only Gammelgaard's counts of direct discourse for the two works in her corpus containing it: Hrabal (Hr) and Placák (Pl), given in 1997:164. One figure — the 67% for the item *můžou* — seems impossible in that it represents only a single token.

64 It is possible that this feature's dual function (see chart 2.3.1) makes it less acceptable in written texts, as its written use is associated with a particular era, genre and register incompatible with modern novelistic dialogue.

some common truncations like *dělaj, sázej* for feature 5, may have more to do with the fact that the acoustic difference represented by the truncated and non-truncated form is relatively slight and difficult to detect; the additional processing effort involved in decoding a non-standard written form like these may not be worth it. Klíma, notably, suppresses many CC forms that are relatively frequent in speech.

The deviations mentioned above may well be grounded in methodological differences and the specific character of literary texts. Kravčišinová and Bednářová's study covered a range of informants speaking on various themes, although educated and public speech was well represented. In literary texts, on the other hand, the number of "informants" is limited to the characters at hand, of which a disproportionate amount will be from the main characters (two to five), and the topics discussed are confined to those that concern the plot and themes of the work. Attempts to give main characters a particular linguistic "profile" may therefore have influenced the data in this study, and may partially explain some of the anomalous results above.

However, consistencies between the three works in their promotion and suppression of certain CC features also deserve attention. The most frequent non-SC variants slot into SC dialogue consistently; the least frequent non-SC variants are excluded entirely. (In Klíma's work, this "least frequent" category is substantially larger.) In two places, we see what is evidently a sharp discrepancy between *real-life frequency* and *aesthetic value* of forms; the relatively frequent form *nes* for feature 9 is demoted sharply, while the relatively infrequent form *vedem* for feature 17 is promoted. This finding suggests that, just as there are discrepancies between speakers' preferences for certain *phonological* forms and their actual usage patterns, there must also be discrepancies between their preferences for certain *morphological* forms and their actual usage patterns. In 5.1, I identified a convergence between overtly expressed value judgments about phonemic variants and novelistic usage of these variants. If this convergence holds for morphology as well, chart 5.2.3 will constitute a model for a morphological hierarchy based on value judgments. Further research that would directly measure speakers' preferences for CC or SC morphological variants could confirm whether those hierarchies also converge in this instance.

A further issue is whether, given the variable frequency and apparent aesthetic value of these variants, we treat them as a single class ("CC"), as is often done. The data suggest at least three groupings of "CC" forms as they relate to dialogue in written texts: frequently used, generally approved features that nonetheless are rarely found in the narrative portions of the novels and do not have the status of full SC variants; somewhat frequent features of medium acceptability that are reflected differently in different works, which are certainly normal for speech but are clearly non-traditional for writing; and forms that may in fact be found with some frequency in speech but are nonetheless stigmatized in writing (and possibly stigmatized in speech as well). This points to a functional distinction between features split at least four ways, rather than the traditional two-way SC–CC distinction.

Comparing the figures from the current study with Gammelgaard's figures proves somewhat less enlightening. In the first place, Gammelgaard's study was not focused primarily on direct discourse, and so her direct discourse statistics are in many places scanty. That fact, combined with the lacunae in my own study, makes it difficult even to find fields across all five works that can profitably be compared. Still, a few points for discussion do emerge clearly.

*1) Promotion of "acceptable" CC features.* Certain features in all works show a high degree of acceptability — typically those acceptable in certain (although not all) types of SC.

*2) Frequency of* bysme (feature 2). None of the texts in this survey have this frequent CC conditional auxiliary; Gammelgaard's corpus does have it in direct discourse, although the numbers are small. Gammelgaard's texts, which use CC forms extensively in narrative discourse, may be more receptive to variants that are frequent in speech and yet aesthetically stigmatized as highly non-standard. If true, this would explain the somewhat elevated usage levels of variants such as feature 10: instrumental plurals in *-ma*, e.g. *pánama*.

*3) Demotion of reduced-effort features.* This seems to be a feature of Hrabal, which demotes CC morphological features that appear to have originated as reductions in or truncations of SC features, specifically *dělaj/sázej* for feature 5, *nes* for feature 9, *vedem* for feature 17. On this point, interestingly enough, Hrabal's usage finds most in common with the relatively literary usage of Klíma. This indicates that breaking down morphological innovations into "reduced-effort" and "analogical" types can be a useful tool for analysis.

*4) Relationships between narrative discourse and direct discourse.* The hierarchies proposed by Gammelgaard for Hrabal's and Placák's direct discourse differ substantially both from those in the current study and from each other. This suggests that the relatively similar hierarchies proposed for the "traditional" modern novel with SC narrative discourse may be upset when narrative discourse is substantially infiltrated by CC features. This sort of comparison introduces another element of aesthetic judgment. We have already noted that when the narrative is in SC, the author's use of non-SC forms is an implicit evaluation of their acceptability in SC discourse. The parameters would, in this analysis, be different if the narrative were not identifiably in SC. Further study of direct discourse in these sorts of works will give a clearer idea of the function of non-SC items.

### 5.3. Syntactic features

While thorough lists of differences between CC and SC syntax can be found, for instance, in Gammelgard 1997:4, syntactic features prove resistant to many sorts of counting or tabulation for a number of reasons.

First, the researcher must decide whether or not to include features that, while clearly part of spoken Czech and claimed to be CC, are cross-linguistically considered to be features of spoken discourse as opposed to written discourse. To take an extreme example, ellipsis is a frequent feature of speech, and thus potentially of CC, although it is not excluded entirely from SC. It occurs in my corpus with some regularity, as in the example below from Kohout:

5.3a     **Že** jste takhle nepsal dřív, nemuseli tu řádit do předloňska
'(Too bad) **that** you didn't write that way before; no reason they had to get their way till last year.'

Should we then count any occurrences of it as "CC?" On reflection, most linguists would disallow this. Ellipsis is an organic outgrowth of real-time speech. If we compare it to other CC vs. SC features, such as the instrumental endings *-ama* and *-ami*, or the phonemes /i:/ and /ɛ:/, we can easily note that these features are assigned to one or the other variety quite arbitrarily; there is nothing in the nature of speech or writing which would dictate that one or the other of the pair must be the CC form or the SC form. This stipulation removes a raft of spoken-language features from consideration as CC features. Many of them, ellipsis included, will be dealt with in the second part of this section instead.

Second, certain other features often labelled "syntactic" are in fact lexical in nature. For instance, the relative pronouns of CC and SC differ, with SC having *který* and *jenž*, while CC uses *k(t)erej* and *co*. Ordinarily the relative pronoun is in the case required by the dependent clause, but *co* is invariable, and a third-person pronoun or other pro-form in the appropriate case is often inserted where an oblique case or prepositional phrase is required.

5.3b    SC:    To je škola,        **do které**    chodí náš syn.
               That is school-NOM **to REL-GEN** goes   our son-NOM

5.3c    CC:    To je škola,        **co   tam**    chodí náš syn.
               That is school-NOM **REL thither** goes our son-NOM

        'That is the school our son goes to.'

5.3d    SC:    To je muž,        **o      kterém** jsme     mluvili.
               That is man-NOM **about REL-LOC** aux-1PL talked-PPL

5.3e    CC:    To je muž,        **co** (j)sme   **vo    něm**    mluvili.
               That is man-NOM **REL** aux-1PL **about him-LOC** talked-PPL

        'That's the man we were talking about.'

The agreement patterns of *o kterém* in 5.3b and *co vo něm* in 5.3c are syntactically different, but can we then treat all differences in relativization as syntactic? Choosing the bookish *jenž* over the neutral *který/kterej/kerej* in 5.3b and 5.3d is more a lexical matter than a syntactic one. At any rate, the choice between these forms does not correspond neatly to the CC–SC opposition, as the latter can be either CC or SC and the former is inappropriately formal in many SC contexts. Classifying the "hard" adjective *který/kterej/kerej* as CC or SC is primarily a phonological, not a syntactic matter, as it involves considering full realization vs. simplification of the consonant cluster /kt/ and appearance of SC vs. CC phonemes in adjectival desinences. Additionally, in some cases (feminine nominative, accusative and instrumental singular) the opposition is neutralized; for example, we cannot say whether *která* (feminine nominative singular) is SC or CC in any given instance, as it is found in both SC and CC.

Third, it is one thing to say that a feature *belongs* to CC syntax and another to say that it *characterizes* CC syntax as against SC, and the same can be said for SC features. Many of the syntactic features cited as CC fall into the former category but not the latter. For example, the use of the preposition *s* 'with' plus the instrumental case to show "instrumentality" (use as a tool) is considered a feature of CC[65], where SC requires the prepositionless instrumental. Examples of this feature are given in 5.3f and 5.3g.

5.3f    Jan píše   s    tužkou.
        Jan writes **with pen-INSTR**

5.3g    Jan píše   **tužkou.**
        Jan writes **pen-INSTR**

        'Jan writes **with a pen.**'

While 5.3f can be labeled CC, it does not follow that ordinary CC discourse only admits this variant; 5.3g would be equally acceptable.[66] Thus, while we can identify certain features as being clearly CC, we cannot identify the remainder of the variations in the set as being SC, making syntactic statistics frustratingly difficult to set in any meaningful context.

Fourth, as Gammelgaard (1997:213) notes, hard data on syntax have been neglected in studies of authentic speech. The paucity of existing studies makes it doubly difficult to assess data about syntax in literature, as we lack a benchmark from speech that can be relied on.

These four factors make syntax much harder to code than morphology or phonology, which has influenced the choice of features coded and discussed in this study.

The more important features coded in this corpus are given in chart 5.3.1 below. A feature (SC or CC variant) had to appear at least once to be in the coding list. Some features from the higher registers of SC were thus absent, as they would not appear in anyone's conversation.

Of the features in chart 5.3.1, the third — use of personal pronouns — proved too unreliable to code. It required too many arbitrary decisions as to whether a given instance represented a truly redundant use of the personal pronoun, or whether it could be justified as an SC usage, as subject pronouns are found in SC in certain accepted contexts (for example, to show emphasis on the subject or contrast with a preceding subject). An impressionistic look at one text (Klíma) seems to indicate a high frequency of redundant personal pronouns, although counting them does not seem particularly productive for the reasons cited above. The use of redundant pronouns could conceivably be the most common CC syntactic feature, and, paradoxically, the difficulty in identifying it as a clearly CC feature may contribute to its prosperity in literary texts.

---

[65]   Notably, Townsend 1990 does not "acknowledge" (i.e. accept as unmarked or ordinary for Spoken Prague Czech) this feature, as some of his informants found it too colloquial (1990:104). In other places as well he is careful to distinguish between acknowledging a syntactic feature for SPC and listing it as the expected or most common variant.

[66]   The situation is not quite parallel to that of morphological features like first-person singular nonpast *pracuju, píšu*. These forms, originally CC, are now accepted for conversational and informal SC, but their usage in SC is limited, both officially and by convention; the forms *pracuji, píši* are still neutral for SC usage.

**Chart 5.3.1. Syntactic features coded**

1) Use of invariable *co* 'what' as a relative pronoun:
   SC* *studenti, kteří tam byli* vs. CC *studenti, co tam byli* 'the students who were there'
2) The "bare instrumental" to signify use of a tool vs. the instrumental with the preposition *s* 'with':
   SC* *psát tužkou* vs. CC *psát s tužkou* 'write with a pen'
3) Predicate nominals in the instrumental case vs. nominative case:
   SC *Jana je učitelkou* vs. CC* *Jana je učitelka* 'Jana is a teacher'
4) Explicit use of personal pronouns where not strictly necessary:
   SC* *přišel* vs. CC *von přišel* 'he came'
5) Subjects reduplicated with third-person pronouns *von, vona, vono, voni*:
   SC* *není to tak strašné* vs. CC *vono to není tak strašný* 'it's not so horrible'
6) Slightly emphatic first singular past-tense forms with a subject pronoun (*já*) and no auxiliary verb (*jsem*):
   SC* *viděl jsem* vs. CC *já viděl* 'I saw'
7) Impersonal sentences with accusative objects vs. nominative objects:
   SC* *bylo slyšet dechovku* vs. CC *byla slyšet dechovka* 'brass band music could be heard'
8) Enclitic *-li* vs. clause-initial *jestli* for 'if':
   SC *je-li doma* vs. CC* *jestli (von) je doma* 'if he's at home'
9) Special possessive forms of personal names vs. genitive of a name indicating possession:
   SC *Viktorovo auto* vs. CC *Viktora auto* 'Viktor's car'

*Variants marked with an asterisk are found in both varieties.*

Chart 5.3.2 below shows the occurrence of the coded syntactic features in the corpus. Several things are notable about these findings.

First, the number of features identifiable as strictly CC or SC is quite low. If considered against the number of utterances in a 30,000-word corpus, they seem to have an impact on only a negligible portion of the text.

Second, contrary to expectation, occurrence of strictly CC forms is lowest in the text with the most CC phonological, morphological and lexical features. As might be expected, however, the most overtly non-standard of the features — the reduplicated subject — is more frequent in Procházková than elsewhere.

Third, Kohout's text has the highest occurrence of strictly SC and strictly CC features, a result that coincides with findings about its marked range in phonology and morphology, and which bears a similarity to the results of my lexical enquiry in 5.4. The relatively frequent occurrence of auxiliary drop in the first person past tense (feature 6) may be explicable in plot terms. Kohout's story takes the form of an investigation; it relies heavily on contradictory accounts of events, revealed through the characters' discussions. This structure may provide more opportunities for such emphatic denials than are encountered in the other works.

Fourth, despite the paucity of CC features in Klíma, CC syntactic feature 1 is prominent. This feature is found frequently in speech, and is markedly non-standard.

**Chart 5.3.2. Occurrence of features in the corpus**

| No. | Feature | Procházková | Kohout | Klíma |
|-----|---------|-------------|--------|-------|
| 1. | relative pronoun | 2 (C) | 16 (C) | 20 (C) |
| 2. | expression of instrument | 0 (C) | 0 (C) | 0 (C) |
| 3. | case of predicate nominal | 3 (S) | 3 (S) | 5 (S) |
| 4. | reduplication of subject | 4 (C) | 3 (C) | 2 (C) |
| 5. | first-person singular auxiliary | 2 (C) | 19 (C) | 4 (C) |
| 6. | case of nominal with infinitive | 1 (C) | 0 (C) | 0 (C) |
| 7. | expression of 'if' | 0 (S) | 5 (S) | 1 (S) |
| 8. | expression of nominal possession | 1 (S) | 5 (S) | 2 (S) |

*(C) = marked or distinguishing variant is strictly CC (other variant used in both codes);*
*(S) = marked or distinguishing variant is strictly SC (other variant used in both codes).*

The numbers in chart 5.3.2 suggest that there are very few clear binary markers of CC and SC syntax in these texts. The fact that we can clearly identify the texts as having syntax characteristic of "distilled" or "cleaned-up" speech is beside the point; syntactically the differences between these texts derive not from code variation, but from register variation and attempts to recreate the spoken medium in print.[67]

An example will serve to illustrate the difference. The imperative is frequently found in these texts (especially in phrases designed to compel attention and involve the interlocutor), so that forms like *poslyš* 'listen', *řekni* 'tell', *pochop* 'try to understand' are far more common than in ordinary narrative text, and impersonal constructions of the sort *je známo* 'it is well-known', which are characteristic of formal written discourse, are infrequent. However, this has nothing to do with the presence or absence of these features in one or another code. SC certainly contains imperatives, even if they are far more frequent in CC. CC certainly does include impersonal constructions of the sort shown above, even if they are not as frequent as in certain sorts of writing. When we posit that constructions found in both varieties are more or less frequent in certain situations, we are discussing register, not code.

Gammelgaard 1997 discusses the syntactic constructions associated with speech and their appearance in underground literature. Her figures also show a typically low occurrence per feature, such that meaningful comparisons between this study and hers are not possible.

Since the occurrence of such "typically CC" and "typically SC" factors is quite low, it makes sense to look not to "on-off switches" that definitely "belong" to one or another code, but to look for quantitative measures. These can be compared to findings in Těšitelová et al. (1987:125-129, 133-136, 141-149), which gives statistics on usage in Czech written texts

---

[67] Gammelgaard (1997:213) states that "linguists who have dealt with CC recognise that at the syntactic level, the borderline goes rather between spoken and written than between CC and LC [Literary Czech, or SC —NB] (Hammer 1985:93, Sgall et al., 1992:129)."

overall. Here we explicitly leave the domain of "codes" and move to one of "registers" within the written language. Among the easily quantifiable factors that can be checked against Těšitelová's statistics are sentence length and ratio of complex to simple sentences. While it could be argued that these are, strictly speaking, stylistic features and not syntactic ones, they subsume a number of more clearly syntactic features, such as the tendency of formal texts to have longer sentences with more subordination. The samples used consisted of the first 1,000 words in each corpus (plus however many words it took to finish the final sentence).

A sentence is a purely graphic unit, and the calculations below reflect this. Any unit ending in a period (.) was taken to represent a full sentence.[68] In practice, this yields sentences like: *Ne.* 'No.' *Nemám.* 'I haven't.' *A ty?* 'And you?' Such short utterances undoubtedly do much to bring down the average length, but the figures in chart 5.3.3 are still remarkably low compared to those for nonfiction texts.

**Chart 5.3.3. Sentence length in written texts**

---

*Dialogue in Czech literary texts:*
Procházková: 208 "sentences" in 1004 words = 4.82 words per sentence
Klíma: 187 "sentences" in 1004 words = 5.36 words per sentence
Kohout: 179 "sentences" in 1001 words = 5.59 words per sentence

*Non-dialogic texts (Těšitelová et al. 1987:142):*
Czech journalistic texts: 16.1 words per sentence
Czech administrative texts: 14.3 words per sentence

---

These figures seem to indicate that the short sentence is a marker of literary dialogue. It also shows a much greater similarity between these three texts than any of the other syntactic features yet examined.

Another quantitative measure of syntactic complexity discussed in both Těšitelová et al. 1987 and Gammelgaard 1997 is the frequency of compound and complex sentences. Czech prose is said to have an approximately equal number of simple sentences vs. complex and compound sentences. This figure is based on samples of both literary and non-literary texts (Těšitelová 1987:145). Of those complex and compound sentences, the greatest number have only two clauses, and the quantities decrease as the number of clauses mount. For this analysis I took an even 200 sentences (slightly more than a thousand words) from each text. Here I counted all sentences where clear ellipsis was present, as in 5.3h:

5.3h     Uklidni se, musíš mi říct, kam mám přijet a co potřebuješ. **Sanitku?** (Kohout)
       'Calm down, you have to tell me where to go and what you need. **A n ambulance?**

---

[68]   Units ending in a comma counted as sentences if they completed a quotation, or were followed by narrative discourse and then a period.

In 5.3h the single-word sentence *Sanitku?* 'An ambulance (accusative singular)?' is elliptical for 'Do you need an ambulance (accusative singular)?' The structure into which the single word fits is clear, and it can be clearly assigned to a sentence type. With sentences of the type found in 5.3i, however, it is hard to know what classification they deserve.

5.3i   „Nerad volám někam, kde to nikdo nebere."
   „Jo? Tak nevolej."
   ' "I don't like calling somewhere where no one picks up."
   "Yeah? Then don't call." '

If we classify *Jo?* 'Yeah?' as a sentence, it could be construed as an elliptical representation of the preceding sentence, in which case it would qualify as a complex sentence, a patently absurd result. Instead, I eliminated these sentences from consideration. Chart 5.3.4 contains the number of sentence types in each text.

**Chart 5.3.4. Simple vs. compound and complex sentences**

| Sentence type | Procházková | Kohout | Klíma |
|---|---|---|---|
| *Simple* | 147 (73.5%) | 135 (67.5%) | 131 (65.5%) |
| *Dependent* | 5 (2.5%) | 2 (1.0%) | 7 (3.5%) |
| ***Subtotal*** | **152 (76.0%)** | **137 (68.5%)** | **138 (69.0%)** |
| *Parataxis 2* | 13 (6.5%) | 19 (9.5%) | 22 (11.0%) |
| *Parataxis 3+* | 2 (1.0%) | 9 (4.5%) | 2 (1.0%) |
| *Hypotaxis 2* | 26 (13.0%) | 16 (8.0%) | 33 (16.5%) |
| *Hypotaxis 3+* | 7 (3.5%) | 19 (9.5%) | 5 (2.5%) |
| ***Subtotal*** | **48 (24.0%)** | **63 (31.5%)** | **62 (31.0%)** |

*Simple = Simple sentence (one independent clause)*
*Dependent = Sentence fragment of one dependent clause*
*Parataxis 2 = Two clauses, parataxis (coordinating conjunction or no conjunction)*
*Parataxis 3+ = Three or more clauses, parataxis only*
*Hypotaxis 2 = Two clauses, hypotaxis (subordinating conjunction)*
*Hypotaxis 3+ = Three or more clauses, at least one subordinating conjunction*

The figures in chart 5.3.4 show that as compared to ordinary written texts, literary dialogue in these three texts has a simple sentence:compound/complex sentence ratio of between 2:1 and 3:1. However, we could take this analysis even further. The statistics in the table above were chosen to match the traditional definition of Czech *souvětí*, which takes in both complex and compound sentences (PMČ 554-555; Těšitelová et al. 1987:150-152). Analyses of written language (Biber 1988, Gammelgaard 1997) show that parataxis vs. hypotaxis (compound vs. complex sentence structure) is a more telling indicator of a text's register. We could thus reformat chart 5.3.4 to reflect this distinction; the result is chart 5.3.5.

**Chart 5.3.5. Simple and compound vs. complex sentences**

| Sentence type | Procházková | Kohout | Klíma |
|---|---|---|---|
| Simple | 147  (73.5%) | 135 (67.5%) | 131 (65.5%) |
| Dependent | 5 (2.5%) | 2 (1.0%) | 7 (3.5%) |
| Parataxis 2 | 13 (6.5%) | 19 (9.5%) | 22 (11.0%) |
| Parataxis 3+ | 2 (1.0%) | 9 (4.5%) | 2 (1.0%) |
| **Subtotal** | **167 (83.5%)** | **165 (82.5%)** | **162 (81.0%)** |
| Hypotaxis 2 | 26 (13.0%) | 16 (8.0%) | 33 (16.5%) |
| Hypotaxis 3+ | 7  (3.5%) | 19 (9.5%) | 5 (2.5%) |
| **Subtotal** | **33 (16.5%)** | **35 (17.5%)** | **38 (19.0%)** |

These figures match Gammelgaard's findings on the sentence structure of underground literature, where she counts the occurrence of hypotactic constructions vs. non-hypotactic ones, yielding figures of between 8% and 27% for four authors. The numbers above — 16.5% to 19.0% — fall in the middle of that range and are remarkably uniform. If excluded connector sentences like *Jo?* 'Yeah?', *Jistě!* 'Sure!' etc. were counted as well in a separate category, the bias against complex (and compound) sentences would be even more noticeable.

Analysis of recorded spoken texts shows a number of syntactic features that are directly attributable to the characteristics of unplanned speech and that are to a certain extent cross-linguistic. Among those treated by Gammelgaard 1997 are: dislocations, repetitions, repairs inside turns, anacoluthon, ellipsis, interruptions and unfinished utterances.

Dislocations have an element removed to a different position in the sentence. In 5.3j and 5.3k the element is dislocated to the right or the left respectively. Gammelgaard (1997:220) points out that dislocations have an impact on the management of topics and informational structure (*aktuální členění věty* 'functional sentence perspective').

5.3j   Však je **to** taky hanba... mít u sebe chlapa a ani si ho nevzít. (Klíma)
       'But **that**'s shameful too, ... to have a fellow living with you and not marry him.'

In 5.3j, the lengthy explanation of what is shameful is dislocated to the right. This preserves the informational structure in which the conversation is "propelled forward" by the introduction of new material or ideas at the end. The dislocation signifies what might in a more formal text be signified by a complex sentence with a subordinating conjunction.

5.3k    Dneska odpoledne tam na sále — ten za kamerou, **to** jsem byl já. (Klíma)
'This afternoon there in the hall — the one behind the camera, **that** was me.'

In 5.3k, the left-dislocated structure, the formulation *ten za kamerou, to jsem byl já* 'the one behind the camera, that was me' moves the known element forward in the sentence such that the final element *já* 'I' is introduced as new information, cf. the possible variant *byl jsem za kamerou* 'I was behind the camera', which informationally locates the speaker in space instead of identifying him with a previously known figure.

Repetition is an occasional feature of these texts. In some instances the repetition is in the information, rather than the words, as in 5.3l.

5.3l    Bolí tě něco? Máš bolesti? (Procházková)
'Does anything hurt? Are you in pain?'

Although the two sentences in 5.3l have different words, they convey almost exactly the same information.

Exact repetition is not infrequent in the corpus. Sometimes the repetition of a phrase is partial, as in 5.3m, where a pregnant girl talks to her mother on the way to the hospital:

5.3m    Před chvilkou **ještě kopal**, cítila jsem ho. Je to sotva pět minut, co **ještě kopal**.
(Procházková)
'A little while ago **he was still kicking**, I felt him. It's barely five minutes since **he was still kicking**.'

Here the two words *ještě kopal* 'he was still kicking' appear in consecutive sentences, in slightly different contexts, linking the second sentence back to the first as a clear modification of its contents. In a similar way, repetition of key words is common in dialogue in consecutive or closely-spaced turns, such that each participant makes clear reference to the part of the preceding turn in formulating a response.

5.3n    "**Takhle** jednáš s každým klukem?"
"Jak **takhle**?" (Procházková)
' "Is **that** the **way** you treat every guy?"
"What's **'that way'**?"

Sometimes the repetition is exact, as in 5.3o.

5.3o    — Jsi má jediná láska, Petruško! ....
— **A ty má. A ty má.** (Kohout)
' "You're my only love, Petruška!"
**"And you're mine. And you're mine."** '

Exact repetition can convey emphasis or strength of emotion. In a written text, other means, including graphic ones — use of space, typeface, capital letters — also play this role.

Repairs within turns, in which a sentence breaks off and restarts either from the beginning or partway through to head in a different direction, indicate confusion or hesitation. In both

planned and unplanned texts, hesitation or confusion can be conveyed explicitly, but the use
of repairs is a feature of unplanned speech only (or of planned speech gone awry). In 5.3p the
author uses a repair to indicate the mother's general agitation at her daughter's plan to cross
the border without a passport, and to underline the mother's realization at the last minute that
she does not know her daughter's boyfriend's name.

5.3p     — Do Mnichova a vůbec za hranice pojedeš až si vyřídíš pas, ale **s tim... jak se
         jmenuje?**
         — Gavros...
         — S tím svým Havrošem dneska můžeš, ale podmínka je, že tě před hranicí někde
         ubytuje... (Kohout)
         ' "You're not going to Munich or abroad at all until you get your passport, **but
         with... what's his name?"**
         "Gavros..."
         "You can go with this Havroš of yours today, but on the condition that he puts you
         up somewhere on this side of the border..."

Sometimes internal repairs are hard to distinguish from anacoluthon, in which a
sentence's structure changes part way through, creating a grammatically awkward or
incoherent utterance, as in 5.3q.

5.3q     Vždycky, když jsme si něco naplánovaly, tak to na něčem zkrachlo, jenže teď'
         najednou se to vyplnilo a máš dceru a... **není to neuvěřitelný?** (Procházková)
         'Always when we'd planned something, then something would go wrong, but now
         suddenly it's come true and you have a daughter and... **isn't it unbelievable?"**

The juxtaposition in 5.3q of a negative question with the train of statements before it has
the character of an unplanned utterance and it is hard to say whether the change is meant to
indicate a correction or merely an awkward change of focus. It is tempting to equate internal
repairs with the appearance of the ellipsis character (...) and anacoluthon with its absence, but
this is not easily provable. A clearer example of anacoluthon is in 5.3r, where the narrator has
a run-in with her lover's father.

5.3r     — Kdo jste??
         — To bych rád věděl o vás, ... — a taky, **kde** na vás Váša bere prachy. (Kohout)
         ' "Who are you??"
         "That's what I'd like to know about you," ... "and also **where** Váša gets the
         money to pay you."

The second clause is apparently an afterthought and involves a second construction with
the verb *vědět* 'know', which sits uneasily with the way it has been used in the first clause.
         Ellipsis is one of the most common features of these texts. As Gammelgaard (1997:222)
points out, the primary difference between standard written ellipsis and conversational ellipsis
is that the former tends to be a form of anaphora, where a previously mentioned referent is
deleted, whereas the latter can also delete other information obvious to participants from the
here and now. To this we could add various elisions of common turns of phrase, such as the

one in 5.3a, which has no immediate referent in the here and now but which would not cause listeners any difficulty in decoding.

Anaphoric ellipsis like that in 5.3s is relatively frequent in these dialogues, but is also a feature of standard written texts:

5.3s    Já totiž potřebuju slyšet, že jsem dobrej, potřebuju to... **jako prase drbání.**
        (Procházková)
        'It's just I need to hear I'm good, I need it... **like a pig** (needs) **scratching.'**

The ellipsis of the verb form *potřebuje* 'needs' in the final clause of 5.3s is easily decoded because the form *potřebuju* 'I need' occurs in the clause before it, also with a direct object *to* 'it'.

In 5.3t an entire clause or logical connection seems to be omitted, but the sense is clear.

5.3t    A když už tam budete, v té jejich anilince prý jde lidem o život. (Klíma)
        'And as long as you're there, supposedly people are dying in their aniline factory.'

The implication of the sentence is: 'And as long as you're there, *have a look at the aniline factory, because....*' This sort of ellipsis mimics unplanned speech, where part of a sentence can stand in for the whole. Ellipsis of this sort can also explain the not infrequent use of dependent clauses standing on their own, as in 5.3u, where a heavily pregnant woman tries to fend off her amorous boyfriend.

5.3u    Když já už se bojím. (Procházková)
        'When I'm already worried.'

The missing clause in 5.3u would be akin to 'that's all I need'.

Interruptions and unfinished utterances are also characteristic of unplanned speech. Examples 5.3v, 5.3w and 5.3x show how this is realized in literary dialogue.

5.3v    A jak ti v tom já... (Kohout)
        'And how can I...'

5.3w    — Československo by nikdy nemohlo dopadnout, jak dopadlo, kdyby se po válce
        ke komunistům nepřesunula jak bahno po průtrži stejná tlustá vrstva lidu, co
        předtím sloužila nácků a udávala třeba zrovna ty parašutisty...
        **— Tím se chlubíš??**
        — ...a která se teď zas nezadržitelně navalila do vašich občanských fór. (Kohout)
        ' "Czechoslovakia never could have ended up the way it did if after the war a
        substantial stratum of people hadn't flooded into the Party like a swamp into a
        ravine, the same stratum that earlier served the Nazis and probably sold out the
        parachutists...
        **"You're proud of this?"**
        "...and that is now pouring unstoppably into your Civic Forum."

5.3x    — A řeklas mu to?
        — Říkám ti, že jsem se s ním ani...
        — ...**nerozloučila.** (Kohout)
        ' "And did you tell him that?"
        "I'm telling you, I didn't even..."
        "...**say good-bye** to him."

In 5.3v we are invited to assume that the character speaking intends to say "and how can I help?" but realizes the question is superfluous, because she already understands what her partner is after. The interruptions in 5.3w and 5.3x manifest the interrupting character's anger, which in the former case results in a question diverting the interruptee's attention, and in the latter results in the speaker irritatedly finishing his interlocutor's turn before trying to get her to answer his question.

Chart 5.3.6 shows the number of sentences in each of the thousand-word samples that exhibit these typical features of unplanned speech.

**Chart 5.3.6. Features of unplanned speech in each sample**

| *Feature* | *Procházková* | *Kohout* | *Klíma* |
|---|---|---|---|
| Dislocations -- right | 0 | 0 | 0 |
| Dislocations -- left | 1 (0.5%) | 1 (0.6%) | 2 (1.1%) |
| Repetition -- full | 1 (0.5%) | 1 (0.6%) | 1 (0.5%) |
| Repetition -- partial | 6 (2.9%) | 1 (0.6%) | 0 |
| Repetition -- semantic | 1 (0.5%) | 2 (1.1%) | 1 (0.5%) |
| Repairs | 3 (1.4%) | 4 (2.2%) | 0 |
| Anacoluthon | 0 | 3 (1.7%) | 2 (1.1%) |
| Ellipsis | 33 (15.9%) | 27 (15.1%) | 30 (16.0%) |
| Unfinished sentences | 1 (0.5%) | 2 (1.1%) | 0 |
| Interruptions | 0 | 1 (0.6%) | 0 |
| Yes/no, appelation | 19 (9.1%) | 16 (8.9%) | 1 (0.5%) |
| Total no. sentences | 208 | 179 | 187 |

If we extrapolate from the sample used in chart 5.3.6 to the entire length of the corpus (approximately ten times the length of the excerpts polled above), then as far as syntax goes, certain features of unplanned speech seem to appear with greater frequency than, for example, features marking the texts as CC. The paucity of explicitly variety-linked syntactic features in the text is compensated for by features associated with the medium and setting (spoken language, unplanned conversations).

## 5.4. Lexical features

It is universally acknowledged among scholars that the lexicon fits poorly into a binary code model. Gammelgaard, for instance, explicitly avoids evaluating and counting individual lexical items on the grounds that too little is known about the layers of the Czech lexicon to make such an endeavor fruitful. Gammelgaard therefore restricted her analysis to the various classes of words that are characteristic of spoken vs. written Czech, such as attitude pointers, politeness routines, hedges, demonstrative pronouns, and so forth (1997:173ff).

It is true that there is no way to count strictly SC vs. CC lexical tokens, as has been done for morphological features, for example. Still, there exist clearly defined categories labelled *spisovné* 'literary' (i.e. standard) and *obecné* 'common' in dictionaries and in handbooks of CC that append wordlists for a CC lexicon. My attempt to find a framework that would allow me to classify the lexicon was thus a necessary exercise, one that was in the end instructive in the light it shed on the SC–CC opposition as a whole.

In collecting and collating data, I relied on three sources. The primary source is the most authoritative source on the Czech lexicon, the eight-volume *Slovník spisovného jazyka českého* (hereafter SSJČ), first published in 1958 and reprinted with minor revisions in 1989.[69] The SSJČ offers a quadripartite "stylistic evaluation" of words and forms. Within it, words are marked according to the features of *spisovnost* 'standardness' (see note below), *frekvence* 'frequency', *dobový výskyt* 'temporal occurrence' and *expresivnost* 'expressivity', but each of these categories is in fact a graded scale, sometimes with with numerous intermediate markers along the way (see chart 5.4.1 below).

Words in the SSJČ are classified where necessary along more than one stylistic axis, so that designations such as *colloquial-ironical, low-expressive-pejorative* and *common-rude-archaic* are among those attached to words in the corpus. Where no designation is given, the word "defaults" to the designation *neutral* or *commonly used* for all axes, as shown in parentheses in the chart. The lack of a secondary or tertiary designation likewise points to a "default" of *neutral* or *commonly used* for any axes not indicated.

The SSJČ classification system presents numerous problems for the researcher. Most of them occur on the standard to non-standard axis described in chart 5.4.1. In the first place, the same criteria have not been used to describe all the terms on the axis. Terms like *journalistic* and *technical* describe a field of work rather than a comment on the acceptability of a word in written texts. In the second place, the criteria are sometimes descriptive, but often prescriptive. The notation *incorrect* for certain forms and terms, to take one example, says nothing about its usage.

---

[69] Another obvious choice would have been the one-volume *Slovník spisovné češtiny pro školu a veřejnost* (SSČ), originally published in 1978 and released in a second, revised edition in 1994. According to Kraus et al. 1982, this dictionary takes a somewhat more permissive attitude toward words previously classed as CC. My choice of the SSJČ instead of the SSČ was eventually based on its more complete coverage of the lexicon and on the perception that it is still the most authoritative dictionary available. The conclusions in this section would have differed little with the use of the SSČ, although more words would undoubtedly have fallen into the category *hovorové* 'colloquial' and fewer into the category *obecné* 'Common Czech'.

**Chart 5.4.1.  Marking of lexical features in the SSJČ**

| spisovnost | standardness[70] | expresivnost | expressivity |
|---|---|---|---|
| knížní | bookish | expresivní | expressive |
| básnické | poetic | familiární | familiar |
| publicistické | journalistic | hanlivé | pejorative |
| odborné | technical | zhrubělé | crude |
| hovorové | colloquial | eufemistické | euphemistic |
| obecné | common Czech | ironické | ironic |
| nářeční | dialectal | (neutrální) | (neutral) |
| oblastní | regional | | |
| lidové | folk | | |
| argotické | argot | | |
| slangové | slang | | |
| nespisovné | non-standard | | |
| nesprávné | incorrect | | |
| (neutrální) | (neutral) | | |
| dobový výskyt | temporal occurrence | frekvence | frequency |
| zanikající | dated | řidší | rarer |
| zaniklé | defunct | řídké | rare |
| zastaralé | obsolete | (běžně užívané) | (commonly used) |
| zastarávající | obsolescent[71] | | |
| (běžně užívané) | (commonly used) | | |

Another difficulty is in interpreting what the terms used in the SSJČ mean.  The authors of the dictionary had a very delicate task in defining these labels, especially in places where the dictionary's normative bent clashed with common usage.  The result is often an uneasy compromise between prescription and acknowledgment of actual usage patterns.  The following paragraphs from the introduction (vol. 1:x-xi) give a good feel for the impossibility of the task the dictionary's authors faced:

---

[70]  More frequently translated as 'literariness' or 'literary character', terms I am avoiding here because of unwanted resonances with the notion of literature as fiction.

[71]  The terms zanikající 'dated' and zaniklé 'defunct' refer to items and concepts no longer in daily use, and whose terms have therefore also taken on a "period" quality.  The terms zastarávající 'obsolescent' and zastaralé 'obsolete' mark words and phrases no longer in daily use, having been superseded by other words or phrases, although their referents are still commonly found.

Ze spisovných slov a spojení se zvlášť označují: h o v o r o v á (zkratka *hovor.*), která se vyskytují obvykle jen v běžně mluvené řeči uživatelů spisovného jazyka, v níž se užívá zčásti též slov obecné češtiny (viz dále).[72]

Contrast this definition with the definition of CC words and expressions found six paragraphs on:

Mezi prostředky spisovného jazyka nepatří sice plně výrazy o b e c n é č e š t i n y (zkratka *ob.*) ale protože části jich se užívá celonárodně v češtině hovorové, nelze je pokládat prostě za nespisovné.[73]

By this definition, then, ColC as a language variety contains words with at least four different usage patterns: those exclusive to SC, but not found in CC; those common to SC and CC; those common to CC and certain spoken varieties of SC (namely ColC); and those not SC but nonetheless found in these varieties of SC speech. However, this typology covers up a lack of functional difference between the last two types. What, after all, is the difference between an SC item not found in SC writing but only in SC speech, and a non-SC item not found in SC writing but found in SC speech? Here no definition of *literariness* or *standardness* will help. The typology itself is its own rationale, and the question remains unanswered.

The SSJČ's equivocation on some points led me to rely where possible on Sgall and Hronek's circumscribed but less prescriptively tendentious lexicon (1992). If Sgall and Hronek gave a different interpretation from the SSJČ, I took their evaluation instead. This added another classificatory term to the already baroque apparatus inherited from the SSJČ. Sgall and Hronek do not use the term *hovorové* 'colloquial', preferring instead the term *běžné* 'ordinary'[74]. Such words in the SSJČ fall into either the category of *colloquial* or *common*. (Sgall and Hronek also have a category headed *common*, meaning strictly CC[75], which contains part of the SSJČ's CC lexicon.)

Items in Sgall and Hronek's classification have a *layer* (*vrstva*) and a *style* (*styl*). Layers include *bookish (knižní), ordinary (běžné), common (obecné), low (nízké), higher and lower slang (vyšší slang, nižší slang). Style* takes care of the more emotional associations attached to words such as *pejorative (pejorativní), familiar (familiární), expressive (expresivní), obsolescent (zastarávající), crude (zhrubělé)*, which are not ranked on a scale.

---

[72] "Among literary words and constructions, those specially marked include: c o l l o q u i a l   C z e c h (abbreviated *hovor.*) words, which usually occur only in the ordinary spoken communication of users of the standard language, where Common Czech words (see below) are also partially used."

[73] "C o m m o n   C z e c h (abbreviated *ob.*) expressions do not fully belong among the standard language's devices, but because some of them are used throughout the country in colloquial Czech, it is not possible simply to consider them nonstandard."

[74] Often translated as 'common', which I avoid here for the obvious reasons.

[75] P. Sgall, personal communication.

These categories are based on (but are not identical to) those found in the SSJČ. If some of the categories in the SSJČ are left to one side as not useful for linguistic analysis, differences between the two approaches can be summarized briefly. The SSJČ takes the written language as its basic form; any forms peculiar to the written language are left unmarked unless noticeably outdated. Spoken forms not acceptable for all forms of literary discourse are marked *colloquial*, and a third layer — *common* — marks those words that are markedly or unacceptably informal when found in SC contexts. Sgall and Hronek have a more descriptive approach that treats the spoken language as the object of study; thus they single out as *bookish* words that are too literary for ordinary conversational usage, and mark a much wider sphere of words as *ordinary* than does the SSJČ, including in this category many words listed in the SSJČ under the more restrictive rubric *common*. It is to be suspected that Sgall and Hronek's definition of *bookish* will also encompass a much wider range of words than that found in the SSJČ. These differences are sketched roughly in chart 5.4.2.

**Chart 5.4.2. Differences in classification of the lexicon**

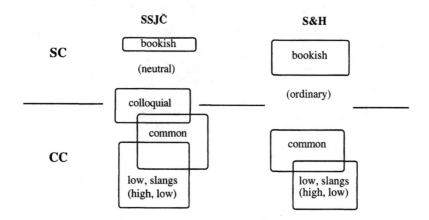

A third source for lexical items was Townsend 1990, which also contains a short lexicon at the end. I only referred to this source when the first two failed to list an item, as it is specifically oriented at Prague Czech and offers no judgments other than membership in a class of words used in Prague Czech.

Despite my use of three sources, thirty-two terms in the three texts (out of a total of 223) either did not appear in any of them, or were marked in such an obviously incorrect manner in the SSJČ (for instance, a frequent contemporary item being marked simply as *defunct*) that I had to set the ruling aside. I chose to regard these words as simply non-SC, under the oft-proven assumption that one way of signalling an item's non-SC status is to exclude it from the dictionary. This approach is consonant with those that treat standard languages like SC as primarily book-defined, rather than speaker-defined.

Despite the SSJČ's acceptance of *colloquial* terms as being SC in some restricted sense, I chose to include them in my counts of non-SC forms. Since they function as full-fledged items outside of SC, but are hedged round with restrictions as to their usage in SC, it made more sense functionally to regard them as "permitted" items that originate in another code or variety. Chart 5.4.3 shows the occurrence of non-SC and SC tokens in the three works. To give an example of my classification strategy: Czech terms for 'father, dad, daddy, papa' include *otec, tatínek, táta, fotr, fotřík*. Of these, tokens of the last three count as non-SC (*táta* is listed as CC and *fotr, fotřík* are slang), while tokens of the first count as SC. The term *tatínek* is neutral, i.e. found in both SC and CC with minimal stylistic and functional limitations, and its tokens were not counted.

**Chart 5.4.3. Non-SC tokens**

| Author | Non-SC tokens | Strictly SC tokens | Appx. word ct.[76] |
|--------|--------------|--------------------|-------------------|
| Procházková | 427 (4.3%) | 104 (1.0%) | 10,000 |
| Kohout | 349 (3.5%) | 55 (0.6%) | 10,000 |
| Klíma | 135 (1.4%) | 85 (0.9%) | 10,000 |
| All texts | 911 (3.0%) | 244 (0.8%) | 30,000 |

Chart 5.4.3 thus provides a fairly complete picture of the amount of vocabulary in each text that can be said to be functionally limited, in other words, that indicates location in a certain variety. Overall, 96.2% of the lexical tokens in these texts are not functionally limited.[77] Of the tokens that are, CC ones outweigh SC ones by factors ranging from 1.5 to 4.3. A relatively small percentage of marked forms therefore suffices to situate literary dialogue in its context for the reader.

We are also interested in the composition of the non-SC vocabulary. Chart 5.4.4 shows non-SC tokens broken down into subcategories (as defined in SSJČ and Sgall & Hronek 1992).

---

[76] The exact total for each text was not recovered. The full word count is between 10,500 and 10,900 words, but this includes sporadic extra words not part of direct dialogue, which were left in to facilitate identification of speakers or situations but were not coded or retrieved during feature analysis.

[77] Some words that are unmarked in the dictionary may in fact be fairly tightly bound to SC and uncommon in other contexts. The word *dívka* 'girl', for example, rarely occurs in unofficial speech, where the word *holka* appears instead, yet the dictionary accords *dívka* no special status. This is a hazard of sticking to dictionary and handbook evaluations, but in these cases, I chose not to stretch my criteria further by adding my own personal opinions where not absolutely necessary.

**Chart 5.4.4.  Stratification of non-SC tokens**

| Layer | Procházková | Kohout | Klíma |
|---|---|---|---|
| colloquial | 56 | 78 | 5 |
| ordinary | 203 | 107 | 95 |
| common | 141 | 110 | 27 |
| dialect/regional | 6 | 1 | 1 |
| low | 5 | 5 | 0 |
| slang | 5 | 14 | 4 |
| undefined | 11 | 34 | 3 |
| **total** | **427** | **349** | **135** |

The vast majority of the tokens in this study fall into the *ordinary* and *common* groups. The so-called *colloquial* stratum also accounts for a healthy number of tokens in at least two of the studies. The number of markedly dialectal, slangy and low-style tokens is remarkably small, constituting less than a tenth of the non-SC tokens, or a tiny proportion of the dialogue sample as a whole. Not surprisingly, I did not find any tokens marked as *poetic, bookish, technical* or *journalistic*; neither did I find any marked as simply *non-standard* or *incorrect*. By and large the non-SC vocabulary in these dialogue texts, then, comes from the "upper" layers of the non-SC lexicon, but most specifically from two layers: the one labeled *ordinary* by Sgall and Hronek and that labeled *common* by the SSJČ. The profile of these tokens, then, might best be described by the SSJČ's equivocative epithet "not wholly non-standard," and the profile of dialogue in these novels overall as "not wholly standard."

A small number of words account for a large number of the tokens. Among the most frequent words attested in the corpus were: *taky* 'also' (125 tokens, layer *ordinary*), *no/nó* 'yes, well' (97 tokens, layer *colloquial*), *jo/jó* 'yeah' (82 tokens, layer *common*), *moc* 'a lot, very, too much' (66 tokens, layer *ordinary*). These words are notably low on semantic content and high on discourse function: they are connectors, attitudinal indicators, and intensifiers. In the next rank, with above 10 tokens in total, were words with some greater semantic content, but low on expressive value: *teda* 'then, so' (27 tokens, layer *ordinary*), *chlap* 'guy, fellow' (20 tokens, layer *ordinary*), *koukat (se)* 'look at' (20 tokens, layer *ordinary*), *holka* 'girl' (14 tokens, layer *ordinary*), *doktor* 'medical doctor' (13 tokens, layer *common*), *ženská* 'woman, lady' (12 tokens, layer *ordinary*). None of the most frequent items were said to have any expressive value.

The vast majority of these oft-repeated tokens came from the *ordinary* layer (284 tokens), with some from the *colloquial* and *common* layers (97 and 95 tokens respectively). If we removed these items from our inventory, the distribution of tokens across the stylistic layers would be more even, and the percentage of non-neutral lexical tokens considerably lower than the already-low level shown in chart 5.4.3.

Non-SC lexical items do not therefore at first blush seem to constitute a numerically significant indicator of "conversationality" with respect to all lexical items in the way that phonological, morphological or syntactic features do. However, it may be unfair to minimize the role of lexical items in this way. We did not figure occurrences of morphological items marked as SC vs. CC against the background of all morphological forms in a text; the many forms that do not participate in any opposition were left out of the equation.

To be fair, then, we should propose a test like the one found in 3.1a, where the importance of the SC–CC divide is demonstrated not by its frequency, but by the existence of points where a choice between SC and CC forms is necessitated. It is precisely this point that defeats the researcher when it comes to the lexicon. Phonological, morphological and syntactic items have been easily counted and pigeonholed as either CC or SC, while lexical items offer an almost endless variety of patterns and possibilities. In contrast to phonology, morphology and syntax, the lexicon has never been presumed to operate on a precisely binary division of forms. An array of functional possibilities exist that make data gathering mind-bogglingly complex. The possibilities given in chart 5.4.5 are among those found in the data.

**Chart 5.4.5. Lexical overlapping: some partial sets**

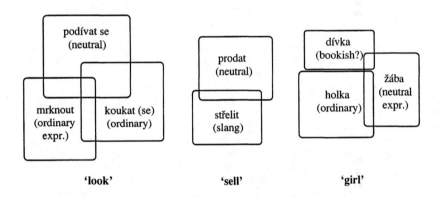

'look'     'sell'     'girl'

How should we count, for instance, the occurrence of a clearly CC form that has a strictly SC equivalent? Does it receive less weight than, or equal weight to, the use of a CC form which has a neutral equivalent? What about a neutral form with a strictly SC equivalent? And how to count the numerous items that participate in a three-way or greater opposition? Any scale developed will of necessity rely on an arbitrary point system for relating degrees of perceived SC-ness or non-SC-ness. For this reason, we may have to stick with the paradox offered by previous research: while the lexicon clearly plays a contributory role, it may prove impossible to measure that role accurately. But this trouble over comparability will lead us back in chapter 7 to the apparently transparent oppositions found in the phonology, morphology and syntax of Czech.

## 6. Profiles of usage

In this chapter I revisit each of the three authors individually and try to establish a linguistic "profile" for direct discourse in their work. I draw on the analysis proposed in 5.1-5.4, while attempting to bring together the various strands of data explored for each work.

Although I chose these three novels for their common features (see chapter 4) rather than their distinguishing ones, they use SC and non-SC features in remarkably divergent ways. Klíma's dialogue is far and away the most standard-sounding of the three; it is rare to find CC phonology in his characters' conversations, although CC verbal morphology and lexical items appear more frequently. The most overt colloquialisms are confined to peripheral characters. Procházková, on the other hand, is by far the closest at reproducing ordinary conversation, making use of a full range of non-SC features for her main characters. In Kohout's work, each character has a clear linguistic profile used to reinforce salient personality traits and peg him or her to a role in the novel. These profiles run the gamut from a relatively high proportion of SC features to one character with virtually no SC features.

### 6.1. Ivan Klíma

Klíma sticks closely to SC phonology, not only in relation to the other authors surveyed, but in an absolute sense as well. The diphthong /ɛj/ as a CC reflex of SC /i:/ (feature E) appears only twice, and then only in stems; /i:/ as a CC reflex of SC /ɛ:/ (feature D) is better represented (14 attestations, or 6.1%), often coming from younger, less educated and more peripheral characters. The rates of attestation are higher for stem occurrences (2/17 or 11.8%) than for desinential occurrences (respectively 9/147 and 3/65, or 6.1% and 4.6%). Initial /vo/ and /ou/ (features F and G) are absent.

The higher rate of attestation in stems for the CC variants /ɛj/ and /i:/ is notable, if only because it suggests that the point at issue is the high acceptability of the CC form in these particular lexical items, and not as a whole. For CC /i:/ (feature D) in stems we find: *oblíct* 'get dressed', *vylítlo* 'flew out'; both of these forms are listed in the dictionary as *common* alongside the SC variants with /ɛ:/: *obléct, obléci* and *vylétlo*. For CC /ɛj/ (feature E) we find: *tejden* 'week' and *prej* 'supposedly' instead of SC forms with /i:/: *týden, prý*; these CC forms too are listed as such in the dictionary under the SC variant. The very existence of these forms in the dictionary must be regarded as some acknowledgment of their growing acceptability, although they are clearly relegated to their place as non-SC variants. All four attestations in Klíma come out of the mouths of secondary characters who are less educated than the main characters.

Klíma does not take every opportunity to use a CC form acknowledged in the SSJČ; sometimes he opts for the conservative SC variant, as in *zahlédl* 'spotted' vs. CC *zahlíd(l)*.

Morphologically, Klíma makes use of more "CC" features, although many of these have gained acceptability within SC, as can be seen in chart 6.1.1 below.

Where a CC form is now acknowledged in SC, Klíma typically uses it instead of the strictly SC variant; thus, first-person singular forms are found with the ending *-ju*: *děkuju* 'I thank'; *uvažuju* 'I am considering'; *ujišťuju* 'I'm checking it out'; *slibuju* 'I promise' (feature

12). Consonantal stem infinitives appear only with the now acknowledged SC/CC ending *-ct* instead of the purely SC ending *-ci*: *oblíct* 'to dress', *říct* 'to say', *moct* 'to be able', never *obléci, říci, moci* (feature 14). Similarly, velar–palatal consonant alternations in the first-person singular and third-person plural (features 7, 8 and 11) are avoided completely.[78] The lower prestige assigned to the CC third-person plural *-jou* (feature 11) is reflected in its lower frequency: *ukazujou* 'they show', *nefungujou* 'they don't work'.

**Chart 6.1.1. CC morphology in Klíma**

---

#můžu 8 (100.0) = #říct 14 (100.0*) = #pracuju 12 (100.0) = #můžou 7 (100.0*)
> lidi 6 (77.3)
> pánama/kostma (32.0)
> pracujou 11 (28.0)
> nes 9 (20.7)
> dobrý auta 3 (14.3)
> dělaj/sázej 5 (0.0) = dobrý hráči 4 (0.0) = vedem 17 (0.0) = prosej(í) 13 (0.0)
= bysme 2 (0.0) = #sází 16 (0.0) = bysem 1 (0.0) = s dobrym 15 (0.0*).

---

There are three clearly non-SC forms that Klíma uses with some frequency. Most frequent are instrumental plural endings in *-ma* (feature 10), which are found in eight out of 25 occurrences for nouns and pronouns (32.0%) and once for adjectives (out of seven occurrences, or 14.3%): *před drátama* 'in front of the wires', *s nima* 'with them', *těma nůžkama* 'with those scissors'. These forms are found in the mouths of main and peripheral characters. Next in frequency is the masculine past participle without *-l* (feature 9); hence we have *přines* 'brought', *odnes* 'took away', *moh* 'could', *nastyd* 'caught cold', *nešáh* 'didn't grab', although for roughly four in five instances (79.3%) the *-l* is retained. The levelling of nominative plural adjectives across all declensions, eliminating the specialized neuter forms (feature 3) in *-á, -a*, occurs in two examples, at a rate of 14.3%: *plně automatizovaný zařízení, ty data* 'fully automated pieces of machinery, those dates'[79]. Both are in the speech of a poorly-educated peripheral character. This levelling does not extend to masculine animate adjectives (feature 4), which retain their separate nominative plural form in all 19 instances, despite the not infrequent levelling of this form in ordinary speech.

Other equally frequent CC features, like first-person plural conditionals in *-bysme* (feature 2) and first-person plural non-past forms in *-em* (feature 17) never appear in this text; neither

---

[78] PMČ regards the older velar forms as "stylově vyšší... vedle dnes již neutrálních forem ... *můžu, můžou*" 'stylistically higher... alongside the forms... *můžu, můžou*, which nowadays are neutral'.

[79] Context suggests a plural reading of *zařízení* here, although the form is identical with the singular. Still, it is less than an unambiguous example.

do apparent regular shortenings in the third-person plural of non-past forms, like *dělaj, uměj* 'they do; they know how' (feature 5).

Klíma makes use of certain accepted CC syntactic features. Well-known CC features like *co* 'what' for the relative pronoun *který, když* 'when' for *jestli* 'if', semantically "empty" use of *to* 'that', and past tense forms without auxiliaries like *já viděl* 'I saw', *já byl* 'I was', *já to uměla* 'I knew how' appear in the text. Given Klíma's generally conservative bent, it is perhaps surprising to see twenty examples of the relative pronoun *co*, far more than occur in the other texts. Features of spoken texts do appear occasionally; those common to written texts, such as ellipsis are more frequent. Anacoluthon, surprisingly, showed up twice in my 1000-word sample, and sentence fragments with dependent clauses were more frequent in this sample than in other authors.

In vocabulary, I found 135 CC tokens (1.4% of the total of 10,000 words), versus 85 uses of SC equivalents (0.9% of the total). These ranged from the relatively neutral use of *dělat* for *pracovat* 'work' or *dneska* for *dnes* 'today' to more stylistically colored or slangy words like *dršťka* 'snout' and *zaflámovat* 'party hard'. Klíma's non-SC vocabulary has only two sources: Hronek and Sgall's *ordinary* layer, with 95 tokens (70.4% of all non-SC tokens) and, to a lesser extent, the CC layer, comprising 27 tokens (20.0% of all non-SC tokens). Slang and so-called "low" words appear only in very small numbers.

Overall, Klíma's dialogue can be taken as a model of what "Colloquial Czech" speech might look like on the page. His main characters use a reasonably pure standard Czech on all levels, but frequently employ permitted variants of SC forms. Non-SC forms seem to mark the speech of peripheral, somewhat less educated characters, often those who appear only briefly and then disappear after a single scene. The lack of CC forms is tempered by the appearance of relatively high numbers of features from impromptu speech, although typically not those that characterize fast or excited speech (repetition, hesitation). The impression created by Klíma's characters is of a certain emotional detachment and distance from each other, sometimes more like a chess game than a human interaction.

## 6.2. Lenka Procházková

In contrast to Klíma, Procházková is considerably more liberal in her use of non-SC variants. Of the three authors, her dialogue generally has the highest percentage of these forms in the text, although she sticks generally to the most popular or accepted forms; many marginal ones find a higher representation in Kohout.

In phonology, the percentage of forms where /ej/ replaces SC /i:/ (feature E) ranges between 45.8% and 68.4%, depending on the phoneme's position in the word; the figures for CC /i:/ replacing SC /ɛ:/ (feature D) is even higher (58.3% to 86.1%). In both instances, CC variants in the stem are least well attested, while non-final desinential CC variants are best attested.

One change that occurs in root-initial position — /vo/ from SC /o/ — is unattested (feature F), and a second — /ou/ from SC /u:/ — is attested only once (feature G). In general, Procházková stays clear of the cluster simplifications and allegro variants attributed to CC, preferring to write *ještě* for *eště*, *nějakej* for *ňákej*, *pojď* for *pod'*, and so forth, although on one occasion each she drops initial *vž-* in *vždycky* and uses the imperative *vem* 'take' instead of SC *vezmi*.

Procházková is equally selective in using CC morphology. Chart 6.2.1 below shows the frequency of non-SC items. Some CC features are used exclusively; these include first-person singular non-past forms in *-ju* and *-Ču* (feature 12: *pracuju, píšu*); elimination of velar alternations in the first-person singular and third-person plural non-past (features 8 and 7: *můžu, můžou*); substitution of nominative plural forms in *-i* for *-ové* (feature 6: *lidi*); and loss of the specialized neuter nominative plural adjective form (feature 3: *dobrý auta*). Other non-SC forms with high frequency in this text (60 to 78.9%) are regularization of third-person plural non-past forms from *-í* to *-ej(í)* (feature 13), truncation in the first-person plural non-past of verbs from *-eme* to *-em* (feature 17), truncation of third-person plural non-past endings in *-ají, -ejí* to *-aj, -ej* (feature 5) and instrumental plural forms in *-ma* (feature 10).

**Chart 6.2.1. CC morphology in Procházková**

---

#můžu 8 (100.0) = #říct 14 (100.0) = #pracuju 12 (100.0) = dobrý auta 3 (100.0*)
= #můžou 7 (100.0*) = lidi 6 (100.0*)
> vedem 17 (78.9)
> prosej(í) 13 (71.4*)
> pánama/kostma 10 (61.1) = dělaj/sázej 5 (60.0)
> pracujou 11 (40.0*)
> nes 9 (33.3) = dobrý hráči 4 (33.3*)
> #sází 16 (0.0*) = s dobrym 15 (0.0*) = bysme 2 (0.0) = bysem 1 (0.0)

---

CC features such as third-person plural non-past forms in *-jou* (feature 11: *pracujou*), *l*-deletion in past participles (feature 9: *nes*) and levelling of the special nominative plural adjective form for masculine adjectives (feature 4: *dobrý hráči*) appear in one-third to two-fifths of all tokens. Absent altogether are non-SC conditional forms like features 1 and 2 (*bysem, bysme* 'I would, we would'), shortening of the final vowel in locative and instrumental singular masculine/neuter adjectives (feature 15: *s dobrym*) and third-person plural non-past extension of the *-í* ending (feature 16: *sází* instead of *sázejí*).

Three of these omissions are unsurprising. The stigmatized character of *bysem* and vowel shortening make them harder to employ convincingly in neutral text. However, the omission of *bysme* (feature 2), which has a relatively high frequency in speech, is notable. Similarly striking in its absence of the third-person plural non-past *-í* ending instead of *-ejí*. This phenomenon, which is found in some Czech dialects, has now been codified into SC. Its absence suggests that codified CC elements, if peripheral or marked in the CC system, will not be adopted for use in literary dialogue.

In syntax, Procházková uses a few token CC features. Sentence-initial *to* and *ono* 'that, it' as dummy subjects are quite frequent, even when syntactically unnecessary; we find sentences like *ono se to třeba vyvrbí* 'it might just work out' or *to seš tak konvenční?* 'are you really so conventional?'. Just under half of all uses of *když* 'when' represent its more conversational concessive or hypothetical meanings 'if, since'. But two standard CC features — *co* 'what' for *který* 'that, which' and deletion of the past tense auxiliary — occur only twice each.

Procházková makes full use of syntactic features of impromptu speech. Sentence fragments beginning with subordinating conjunctions occurred five times in my sample of 200 sentences; other features well representend were ellipsis and repetition. Some dislocations were also found.

Procházková's vocabulary has a markedly non-SC flavor; I found 427 tokens (4.3%) that are not fully SC, extending from the *ordinary* layer down into what Hronek and Sgall call "low" CC, with words like *búr* 'tenner', *dědula* 'old guy', *cimra* 'room' and slang like *střelit* 'sell'. Of the non-SC tokens, almost half (203 tokens, with 49 representing *taky* 'also') come from the *ordinary* layer, with a further 56 from the *colloquial* layer (mostly tokens of *no, nó* ', yeah, well'). A total of 141 tokens fall into the CC layer, with 57 of those representing *jo, jó* 'yeah'. Some stylistically neutral conversational features appear to the exclusion of their fully SC counterparts; among these are *radši* 'rather', *holka* 'girl', *chlap* 'guy', *doktor* 'doctor'. Others are more complex; there are 11 examples of *koukat/nakouknout* 'look', with four examples of *dívat se/podívat se*.

Overall, Procházková comes close to using CC as a neutral code for dialogue. She delimits it fairly sharply, accepting some features completely, varying her use of a second class of features and excluding a raft of more stigmatized features, including phonological, morphological, syntactic and lexical items. The degrees of usage seem to correspond more closely to aesthetic judgments about CC items than they do to actual usage in speech.

## 6.3. Pavel Kohout

Kohout's usage patterns seem at first to fall between those of Klíma and Procházková. Upon closer examination, we find substantial differentiation between the largish cast of major characters that may have a bearing on how we interpret the data.

Phonemically, Kohout's characters show a marked preference for SC forms, although CC forms are well in evidence. The diphthong /ɛj/ appears in place of SC /i:/ (feature E) in anywhere from 2 in 5 to 1 in 12 occurrences, depending on position. The most common place for /ɛj/ is in desinence-final position (40.2%), followed by position in the stem (26.3%). Non-final position in the desinence is relatively rare (6.3% of instances). The phoneme /i:/ in place of SC /ɛ:/ (feature D) is somewhat more consistent, appearing in 36-39% of occurrences across the board. These features appear in the speech of all characters, although they are most common in that of peripheral ones, and they do penetrate all the way up to the speech of the narrator and her current lover, who by and large use SC forms. They are especially common in the speech of the narrator's former lover, a lawyer by training, who worked for the secret police during the Communist years; and the narrator's daughter (see below).

Unlike the other texts, which largely avoid the use of word- and root-initial /vo/ (feature F), both these features appear in Kohout, albeit at low frequencies. Word-initial /vo/ (F1) appears in 38 of 280 tokens (13.6%), while at root-root boundaries (F2) it occurs in one of six tokens (16.7%). (If dialectal *zvostal* 'stayed' as a variant of SC *zůstal* is counted in the latter figure, it rises to 4 in 9 (44.4%).) These features only occur in the speech of peripheral, less educated characters, including the narrator's daughter, who is a caricature of modern youth.

As mentioned in 5.1, Kohout is the only author surveyed to make even occasional use of the "disputed" phonological features of CC, such as consonant cluster simplification and lengthened/shortened vowels. These explicitly indicated pronunciations are by and large limited to the narrator's wayward teenage daughter and the uneducated working-class family of her ex-lover, who live in Kladno, an industrial city thirty miles from Prague. I found only three examples of these non-standard written variants in the lines of the three main characters (*vem* 'take (imperative)' for SC *vezmi* and *osum, osumdesát* 'eight, eighty' for SC *osm, osmdesát*), and of these, the last two are stylizations, since [osum] is now a widespread codified SC pronunciation for written *osm.*

The question thus arises as to whether these spellings are meant to give us extralinguistic, rather than strictly linguistic, information about how the characters speak. A good example is the spelling of words that begin with *j-* plus a further consonant in SC. In spoken Czech, the pronunciation of word-initial /j/ before a consonant is, in many environments, archaic or a feature of exceedingly careful speech. Thus, most non-past forms of the verb *být* 'be' are ordinarily pronounced with the initial /j/ dropped, i.e. *jsem, jsi, jsme, jste, jsou* are pronounced as [sɛm, sɪ, smɛ, stɛ, sou], and not as [jsɛm, jsɪ, jsmɛ, jstɛ, jsou]. This pronunciation is acceptable for spoken SC, and is not confined to CC.[80] Interestingly enough, when reporting teenage speech; Kohout usually writes *sem, sme* for the narrator's daughter in contrast to her mother, for whom he writes *jsem, jsme, jste.*[81] Additionally, CC has an alternate second-person singular form for the verb, based on analogy to regular verb conjugations where the second person singular ends in -*š* /ʃ/: [sɛʃ] 'you are'. We can thus imagine two possible spellings for it: one (*seš*) that reflects phonetic reality, and one (*jseš*) that graphically identifies it as a member of the SC paradigm of the verb 'to be'. Kohout uses both spellings, distributing them to different characters. For the mother he writes *jseš*, a mix of SC phonology and CC morphology, while for the daughter he writes *seš*. He may not necessarily be suggesting that the mother is saying [jsɛʃ] in most of these situations, as in many of them there is no preceding vowel to prompt the realization of the initial /j/ (e.g. *Jseš tam?* 'Are you there?'). Instead, he is aligning the mother with a certain sort of more careful speech pattern, and the daughter with an exceptionally sloppy one. Rather than suggesting any necessary difference in pronunciation, the presence or absence of *j-* in the spelling of these words (and others like *jméno* 'name', *jde* 'goes') is a marker of linguistic status.

A list of these quasi-phonetic spellings found in the corpus is given in chart 6.3.1, classified by type.[82]

---

[80] After a vowel the /j/ may be pronounced if liaison occurs: *nejsme* 'we are not' is always [nɛjsmɛ], while *ale jsme* 'but we are' is [alɛsmɛ] or [alɛjsmɛ].

[81] This j-drop is not applied universally to the daughter's speech, although it does occur in a vast majority of instances.

[82] By *quasi-phonetic* I mean that Kohout makes explicit some pronunciations that may be standard but deviate from ordinary spelling practice (e.g. omission of "silent" letters, insertion of epenthetic vowels). His orthography rarely disrupts the normal morphophonemic character of Czech spelling in the way that Svoboda's does, e.g., he does not indicate routine voicing assimilation or final devoicing in his spellings. To take an example, Kohout does indicate the non-standard vowel length in *polívku* (/polɪvku/ vs. SC /polɛːvku/ or non-SC /poliːvku/ 'soup') but does not indicate the voicing assimilation of /v/ to [f] before the unvoiced /k/ that would yield the actual pronunciation [polɪfku]. This voicing assimilation is found in all major register and dialect varieties of Czech.

**Chart 6.3.1.  Quasi-phonetic spellings in Kohout**

| quasi-phonetic | IPA | gloss | # | usually spelled | IPA | # |
|---|---|---|---|---|---|---|
| **lengthened** | | | | | | |
| *ahój | aɦoːj | hi | 1 | ahoj | aɦoj | 3 |
| *jó | joː | yeah | 10 | jo (not SC) | jo | 18 |
| *né | nɛː | no | 8 | ne | nɛ | 45 |
| *vodevříno | vodevr̝iːno | open | 1 | otevřeno | (ʔ)otɛvr̝eno | -- |
| *vědít | vjɛɟiːt | know | 1 | vědět | vjɛɟet | 5 |
| *zavříno | zavr̝iːno | closed | 1 | zavřeno | zavr̝eno | 1 |
| **shortened** | | | | | | |
| *dolu | dolu | down | 1 | dolů | doluː | 1 |
| *(ne)muže | (nɛ)muʒɛ | can(not) | 2 | (ne)může | (nɛ)muːʒɛ | 44 |
| *neni | nɛnɪ | is not | 1 | není | nɛniː | 16 |
| *nevim | nɛvɪm | I don't know | 1 | nevím | nɛviːm | 4 |
| *(s) nim | s nɪm | him (instr.) | 1 | (s) ním | s niːm | 11 |
| *polivku* | polɪfku | soup | 1 | polévku (-í-) | polɛːfku, -iː- | -- |
| *prosim | prosɪm | please | 1 | prosím | prosiːm | 20 |
| **both** | | | | | | |
| *zéli* | zɛːlɪ | cabbage | 1 | zelí | zɛliː | 1 |
| **clusters** | | | | | | |
| *cerku | t͡serku | daughter/girl | 1 | dcerku | tserku | 8 |
| *dyť | dɪc | after all | 6 | vždyť | vʒdyc | 3 |
| *dyž | dɪʃ | when | 4 | když | gdɪʃ | 38 |
| *jesli | jeslɪ | if | 3 | jestli | jestlɪ | 12 |
| *kerá | kɛraː | which | 1 | která | ktɛraː | 30 |
| *ňák- (-ý...) | ɲaːk- | some | 5 | nějakou, -ý | ɲɛjak- | 3 |
| *páč | paːt͡ʃ | because | 1 | protože | protoʒɛ | 9 |
| *pod' | poc | come! | 1 | pojd' | pojc | -- |
| *rači | rat͡ʃɪ | rather | 3 | radši | rat͡ʃɪ | 3 |
| sem | sɛm | I am | 14 | jsem | sɛm, jsɛm | 164 |
| si | sɪ | you are (sg.) | 1 | jsi | sɪ, jsɪ | 43 |
| sme | smɛ | we are | 5 | jsme | smɛ, jsmɛ | 23 |
| sou | sou | they are | 1 | jsou | sou, jsou | 4 |
| ste | stɛ | you are | 1 | jste | stɛ, jstɛ | 37 |
| vem | vɛm | take! | 1 | vezmi | vɛzmɪ | 1 |
| **other** | | | | | | |
| eště | ɛʃcɛ | still | 3 | ještě | jeʃcɛ | 12 |
| *Jozef | jozɛf | Joseph | 2 | Josef | josɛf | 8 |
| -osum- | [v]osum | eight | 2 | -osm- | (ʔ)osm, (ʔ)osum | 3 |
| *porád | poraːt | continuously | 1 | pořád | por̝aːt | 6 |

In chart 6.3.1, "lengthened" includes examples where the attested variant has a longer vowel than the usual (most often SC, but sometimes CC) variant, and "shortened" subsumes examples where the attested form has a shorter vowel than the usual variant. The single form under "both" has a long vowel for a usual short vowel, and a short vowel for the usual long vowel. "Clusters" takes in examples where the attested variant has a simplified consonant cluster, compared to the usual form. "Other" contains random differences between the usual and attested forms, including initial consonant truncation (*eště* vs. *ještě*), differences in voicing and articulation (*Jozef* vs. *Josef*; *porád* vs. *pořád*) and epenthetic vowels (*-osum-* vs. *-osm-*).

As can be seen from the chart, most of the quasi-phonetic spellings correspond to standardized (either SC or conventional CC) spellings found elsewhere in the dialogue. For some words, individual characters have a "profile" of using either the quasi-phonetic spelling or the usual spelling, while for other words (*osum* vs. *osm*; *sme* vs. *jsme*; *porád* vs. *pořád*) both spellings are used in the same character's lines.

It is also interesting to note the distinct functional differences represented by different pairs in chart 6.3.1. As mentioned above, some of these quasi-phonetic spellings do not indicate a necessary divergence from CC or even SC pronunciation.[83] On the other hand, some of the spellings (those given in italics in chart 6.3.1, like *polivku* and *zéli*) indicate idiolect or dialect pronunciation, and would be noticed as such by CC speakers. Two further categories comprise the rest of the list. In the first, the phonetic pronunciation does represent what we could term ordinary CC pronunciation (e.g. *eště* for *ještě*; *vem* for *vezmi*). In the second, and much larger, category, marked by an asterisk in the first column, the pronunciation indicated is a deviation from "normal" CC. For these asterisked forms, then, what is indicated is some sort of "sub-non-standard" pronunciation.

These "sub-non-standard" pronunciations are mostly found in the speech of the narrator's daughter and her lover's Kladno family. In the case of the narrator's daughter, there is a clear attempt to represent all pronunciation quasi-phonetically, as it is more or less consistent and is accompanied by the "phonetic" spellings discussed above that represent SC pronunciation. In the case of the Kladno family, these "phonetic" spellings are most often accompanied by standard spellings of words like *jsme* 'we are' *když* 'when, if', *říkat* 'say' and not the non-standard *sme, dyž, řikat*, although the speech of one character, a grandmother, contains some of these markedly non-standard forms.

A literary analysis focusing on the traits of various characters would be necessary to explain fully why the forms have this particular distribution among the characters. In any event, these quasi-phonetic spellings are characteristic of minor characters, and although some of these spellings do not tell us that a particular character pronounces a word in an unusual way, the overall effect of them does contribute to characterization.

Furthermore, although all the spellings in chart 6.3.1 are non-standard, there are very few of them that indicate the use of CC in a neutral sense. Most point to a particular "lower" variety of CC or seem to redundantly indicate pronunciations that are now considered

---

83  Particularly interesting in this regard is the spelling *rači* for *radši* 'rather'. Note that we can distinguish these forms *phonemically* using an IPA transcription, but that the presence or absence of a tied bar is unlikely to show up in speech.

standard. The use of these non-standard spellings cannot thus be taken as the author's way of indicating the use of mainstream, unmarked CC.

In morphology, Kohout shows a marked but not exclusive preference for standard forms, as can be seen in chart 6.3.2 below.

CC forms appear at 100% frequency for only three features. Infinitives of consonant-stem verbs (feature 14) appear as *říct, utéct, pomoct* 'to say, to flee, to help', and never *říci*, etc. Likewise, Kohout always gives preference to the non-standard nominative plural form in *-i* over SC *-é* (feature 6). Slightly surprisingly, the third-person plural *mohou* type (feature 7) gives way completely to the analogically rebuilt form like *můžou*, while the more acceptable first-person singular form *mohu* retains some currency alongside CC *můžu* (feature 8).

**Chart 6.3.2. CC morphology in Kohout**

---

lidi 6 (100.0*) = #říct 14 (100.0) = #můžou 7 (100.0*)
> #pracuju 12 (92.9)
> vedem 17 (88.9)
> pracujou 11 (75.0*)
> dobrý auta 3 (66.7*)
> dobrý hráči 4 (60.0)
> #můžu 8 (58.3)
> pánama/kostma (44.0)
> nes 9 (39.0)
> prosej(í) 13 (26.7)
> s dobrym 15 (10.0)
> dělaj/sázej 5 (5.3)
> bysem 1 (3.0)
> bysme 2 (0.0*) = #sází 16 (0.0*)

---

The CC forms appearing most frequently are analogical first-person singular non-past forms in -u (feature 12), like *miluju* 'I love', *zdržuju* 'I detain', truncated first-person plural forms (feature 17), like *projedem* 'we'll drive through', *neobviňujem* 'we do not accuse', *mrknem* 'we'll have a look'; 88.9% to 92.9% of both types appeared in the CC form. Levelling of nominative plural adjectives (features 3 and 4) is not uncommon. Sixty percent of the masculine animate tokens show levelling, while two-thirds of neuters show levelling).

At slightly lower frequencies are CC instrumental plural forms in *-ma* (feature 10: 44.0%). Truncated masculine past participles (feature 9) appear in two of five occurrences, and I found CC third-person plural forms *-ěj(í)/-ej(í)* (feature 13) in more than one in four instances (CC *zvoněj* 'they ring' *tvořej* 'they make up' *myslej* 'they think', *jezděj* 'they come' instead of SC *zvoní, tvoří, myslí, jezdí*). There were two single forms with under a 10% rating: the substandard first-person singular conditional auxiliary *bysem* (feature 1) and the truncated third-person plural form *kálej* (SC *kálejí*) 'they defacate' for feature 5.

Syntactically, Kohout's characters have a similarly eclectic profile. Of the SC and CC features in the text, Kohout has the highest occurrence of both overall. These are to a certain extent distributed among the socially diverse cast of characters. Kohout makes frequent use of features of impromptu speech; my 1000-word sample contained four repairs and three examples of anacoluthon, as well as an interruption and two unfinished sentences, repetitions and a left dislocation. The frequent use of these features highlights the extent to which the plot of the novel revolves around verbal interrogations, and the surprises and misunderstandings that they cause.

There is a strict hierarchy of usage in Kohout's novel. The heroine and her lover speak more or less SC, although with a liberal sprinkling of non-SC lexemes; their linguistic profile looks much like the profile of Klíma's characters. One character, a secret policeman of proletarian background, has a less standard speech pattern. On the other end of the scale, the heroine's high-school-age daughter is responsible for half or more of the CC elements in the novel. Minor characters in Kohout's novel tend to appear as caricatures, and several of them use CC as well. The effect of this is quite persistent, and has the appearance of a literary conceit.

# 7. Revisiting the SC-CC interface

In this chapter I will revisit some of the more relevant investigations discussed earlier and see how they can help in developing a different model for the SC-CC interface — one that will describe how dialogue is written in literary texts.

The amount of data and its diversity make several interpretations possible, of which I will mention two: those which support the current model of CC and SC as competing codes within the Czech language, and those which argue for a less binary approach.

First, we could look at the data as supporting the claim for two competing codes. In this account, representing spoken communication in a literary work is a problematic area, because the usage spheres of the two codes intersect at this point. The author of a novel written in garden-variety SC cannot consistently use SC forms to represent speech, because they are not appropriate to its content or tone. On the other hand, he also cannot consistently choose CC forms, because doing so forfeits the text's status as a SC document. (See Cummins 1994 for a fuller discussion of these issues.) In a text with a mixture of CC and SC forms, the characters keep their status as SC personages, while their conversation retains a semblance of naturalness it would otherwise lack. This presupposes a certain interconvertability between two coexisting codes, and the reader's ability to sort out these doublets as a natural and automatic feature of text processing.

Running counter to this argument is the intricate structure of the SC–CC distinction. A number of studies, including the current one, cast doubt on the broad, binary interpretation often given to the labels "CC" and "SC". Those studies focusing on "aesthetic value" of features suggest the existence of hierarchies, in which individual variants are more or less "acceptable" in given circumstances. Those focusing on actual usage patterns in speech show a broadly similar hierarchy of "more" and "less employed" forms, although the details and actual frequencies differ from the aesthetic-value studies. It is unclear, then, how useful the labels "SC" and "CC" are to us for individual variants, since they reflect neither the actual frequency of usage nor the values native speakers assign to these forms. It might, in the end, be more appropriate to sort the linguistic variants involved into groups, and to determine the character of the text by reference to which groups of variants it employs. The resulting pattern will look more like a scale of register variation, with texts arrayed on a cline from SC to CC by virtue of the occurrence of certain groups of features. In this analysis, we will still have varieties at either end of the scale called "SC" and "CC", but we will not use these terms to label individual forms.

## 7.1. Validity of phonemic hierarchies

In chapter 5 we saw that Kučera's expectations of acceptability are by and large borne out in the frequency counts for these works. There are also rough but general similarities with the frequency counts found for phonemic changes by Kravčišinová and Bednářová 1968 and by Gammelgaard 1997. Although the numbers are different, the general ordering of frequency and acceptability are the same.

Do these hierarchies translate into specific constraints on usage proposed by Kučera and confirmed by Gammelgaard? Here my findings partially support Kučera's, but in the main are closer to those of Kravčišinová and Bednářová, which found very few constraints operating on any level larger than that of the single word. In other words, while the hierarchies do seem to accurately reflect the frequency of items in literary dialogue, they cannot be generalized into a set of rules by which the appearance of one feature automatically blocks or conditions the appearance of another outside the phonological word.

Kučera proposed that the acceptability hierarchy he found imposed constraints on the use of CC and SC phonemic features. If an item low on the CC acceptability hierarchy was employed, then all higher-ranked items in the vicinity also had to be employed. We can test these texts against Kučera's hierarchy and against the hierarchies implied by the texts themselves to see how valid they are.

**Chart 3.4.1. (Repeated.) Kučera 1955**

---

*Frequency and hierarchy of CC phonemes, percentages:*

|   | | |
|---|---|---|
| i: (84.8; 78.2) | feature D |
| > -ɛjC/-ɛj (83.5; 70.6) | features E2, E1 |
| > -ɛj- (60.1; 36.7) | feature E3 |
| > #vo (42.9; 20.9) | feature F |
| > #ou (22.9; 7.6) | feature G |

---

Some examples in these texts clearly support Kučera's hierarchy:

7.1a.   Vypomáhám generálnímu komisaři **rakouskýho** průmyslu vyznat se ve zdejších **daňových** předpisech, **kterým** zatím nerozumí ani náš pan ministr financí. (Kohout)
'I'm helping the **Austrian** (CC) general commissar of industry to figure out the local **tax** (SC) codes, **which** (SC) even our finance minister doesn't understand.'

In 7.1a, the CC form /iːfio/ for SC /ɛːfio/ (genitive singular adjective ending; feature D2) is present, while the SC forms /iːx/, /iːm/ occur instead of their CC counterparts, /ɛjx/, /ɛjm/ (locative and dative plural adjective endings; feature E2). Since /#vo/ (feature F) is found only in Kohout, and at that in the speech of a teenager who uses CC consistently, this is almost a foregone conclusion. The CC variant /#ou/ (feature G) occurs only once, in Procházková (see 7.1b below), and there are no other telltale phonemic features in the vicinity. The nearest marked feature is *víc* 'more', which is far enough away syntactically and temporally to be outside Kučera's frame of reference.

7.1b    Ty se přece vyznáš v **ouřadech** a těchhle ‚konvenčních pitominách' **víc** jak já.
        (Procházková)
        'You know your way around **offices** (CC) and those "conventional idiocies" **more**
        (CC) than I do.'

However, there are numerous examples of Kučera's phonemic hierarchy being violated as well. One can be seen in 7.1c:

7.1c    **Idiotské** poznámky **pitomejch** nemá cenu poslouchat.
        'There's no point listening to **stupid** (SC) people's **idiotic** (CC) remarks.'
        (Procházková)

Here the SC variant /ɛ:/ appears in the word *idiotské* 'idiotic', while two words later, in the same noun phrase the CC variant /ɛj/ appears in *pitomejch* 'stupid (people)'. This contravenes Kučera's 1955 hierarchy in that the presence of the CC form in the latter word should condition the presence of the CC form *idiotský* in the former. This particular hierarchy thus does not seem to bear up if applied on a scale larger than that of the single word.

A second phonemic hierarchy claim made by Kučera was that CC forms in adjectival endings can combine with SC forms in roots, but not vice-versa (see Kučera 1958:186-187 and 3.5 above). I found only three examples, all from Procházková and with the same adjective. Here, the presence of /ɛj/ in the root (feature E3) seems in fact to require CC forms in the endings (feature E2) as well, hence *bejvalejm, bejvalej, bejvalejma* 'former (dative plural, masculine nominative singular, instrumental plural)' but not *\*bejvalým, \*bejvalý, \*bejvalýma* with CC phonemes in the root and SC phonemes in the ending. Interestingly enough, Kučera later removed this constraint from his list (see Kučera 1973:518).

## 7.2. Relevance of morphology-related hierarchies

Kučera originally proposed that if CC phonological features were realized in a segment, then CC morphological features had to be realized there as well. A prominent example is the instrumental plural adjective form, which contains a segment with both CC and SC phonemic variants, adjacent to a desinence with both CC and SC forms. Chart 3.5.2 shows the four possibilities that obtain.

**Chart 3.5.2. (Repeated.) The instrumental plural adjective ending**

|                      | SC vowel /i:/ (E2)   | CC vowel /ɛj/ (E2)   |
| -------------------- | -------------------- | -------------------- |
| SC morph -*mi* (10)  | –*ými* /i:mɪ/        | *\*-ejmi* /ɛjmɪ/     |
| CC morph -*ma* (10)  | -*ýma* /i:ma/        | -*ejma* /ɛjma/       |

According to Kučera 1958, we will find the thoroughly SC form –*ými* (/i:mɪ/) as well as the thoroughly CC form -*ejma* (/ɛjma/). Of the other possibilities, only the one with CC morphology and SC phonology, namely *-ýma* (/iːma/) is acceptable. The form with SC morphology and CC phonology, *-ejmi* (/ɛjmɪ/) is not acceptable. This general statement was later refined into an examination of six morphology-phonology intersections, discussed at greater length in 3.5.

Unfortunately, the extreme bookishness of some of the forms limits their relevance to this corpus. We require highly specific environments to test Kučera's claims, and the corpus provided them only rarely — certainly not in enough quantities to say conclusively that certain forms "can" or "cannot" appear.

In chart 7.2.1, Kučera's hypothesis is laid out in the first four columns. The corpus examples are in the sixth column, and the limited conclusions that can be drawn from the corpus examples are in the fifth column.

**Chart 7.2.1.  Kučera's morphology hierarchies in the corpus**

| Combinations | P | M | Hypothesis | This corpus | Corpus examples | Labels |
|---|---|---|---|---|---|---|
| -ými | SC | SC | | attested | americkými, jakými, | E2 + 10 |
| -ejma | CC | CC | | attested | zrazenými, tvejma, | |
| -ýma | SC | CC | | not attested | bejvalejma, přepych- | |
| *-ejmi | CC | SC | ruled out | not attested | ovými, nadhernými, malými, chytrými, starými, rozepjatými | |
| bíti/péci | SC | SC | | not attested | oblíct, bejt (6x), | E3/F3 |
| bejt/píct | CC | CC | | attested | pobejt, umejt, být | + 14 or -t(i) |
| bít/péct | SC | CC | | attested | (36x), nebýt, výt, | infinitive |
| *bejti/*píci | CC | SC | ruled out | not attested | zakrýt | |
| otekou | SC | SC | | not attested | none | F1 + 7 |
| votečou | CC | CC | | not attested | | |
| otečou | SC | CC | | not attested | | |
| *votekou | CC | SC | ruled out | not attested | | |
| osvobozují | SC | SC | | attested | obstupují, obsluhujou, | F1 + 11 |
| vosvobozujou | CC | CC | | not attested | obdivujou | |
| osvobozujou | SC | CC | | attested | | |
| ?vosvobozují | CC | SC | doubtful | not attested | | |
| létají | SC | SC | | attested | slévají se (2) | D3 + 5 |
| lítaj | CC | CC | | not attested | | |
| *létaj | SC | CC | ruled out | not attested | | |
| lítají | CC | SC | | not attested | | |

P = phonology; M = morphology

Despite the limited data available in chart 7.2.1, it is noteworthy that none of Kučera's hierarchies are violated in the corpus. We can observe all three of Kučera's permitted patterns: SC phonology plus SC morphology; CC phonology plus CC morphology; and SC phonology plus CC morphology, but never CC phonology plus SC morphology.

Interestingly enough, these patterns are not distributed evenly across the various environments. Instead, some environments favor consistent use of either SC or CC forms, while one context is only found with SC phonology, although both CC and SC morphology appear. This suggests that, rather than being a hard-and-fast rule governing the combination of morphological and phonological elements as Kučera first supposed, the elements are best treated as individual items arranged in a hierarchy of acceptability that influences the way they combine with each other.

### 7.3. Applicability of code-switching models

Much of the research on code-switching has little relevance for constructed texts, which come into being in a completely different way from ordinary spoken discourse does. In particular, models that rely on psycholinguistic structures, such as Scotton's Matrix Language Frame model, will prove completely beyond the scope of this study. The work of a writer drafting and revising a written conversation at a desk is completely different from the real-time processing of language between participants in a spoken interchange, and it is unreasonable to expect these texts to shed much light on such theories, or conversely for the theories to be applied to texts constructed under completely different conditions.

What makes certain types of code-switching research applicable to these texts is the fact that the texts are presumably intended by their authors as believable representations of speech, and as such they should not seem implausible to native speakers accustomed to the same interaction of varieties in their own speech. Authors presumably take care to make sure that their characters' speech gives an accurate portrait of their mental makeup and evolving emotional state, and that interactions between characters reflect their setting and tone. Theories which address readily observable internal or external situations (the relationship between participants; the setting for a conversation; the emotional state of participants) thus provide the best ground on which examine whether or not literary texts exhibit code-switching in the same manner as spontaneous interchanges.

As mentioned earlier, a code-switching model of Czech, in which two coexisting codes are employed, allows us to identify two types of switches from code to code: *situational* and *communicative*. Applied to Czech, these types would allow code-switching in the following places.

Situational code switches should occur when the mode of discourse changed in some way. For Czech, we are likely to posit that the standard code will occur in public situations (public addresses, classrooms, television and radio discourse, except where an intimate effect is deliberately being created) and situations where people converse as representatives of corporate organs. The non-standard code will occur in situations marked as familiar, intimate, or informal. Conversations with family and friends will be in the non-standard code; workplace conversations where people act as individuals rather than as representatives are likely to be non-standard as well.

Communicative code-switching states that "within" the established domains of codes, further switching will occur. Two sorts of models have been proposed for these code switches: *pragmatic motivators* and *structural constraints*.

In studies concentrating on pragmatic motivators, researchers try to determine what non-syntactic features of a conversation can prompt a switch in code. Auer 1995 brings together a list of communicative points when code-switching occurs, found in chart 7.3.1.

## Chart 7.3.1. Communicative code-switching "triggers" (Auer 1995)

Reported speech
Change of participant constellation
Parentheses or side-comments
Reiterations (quasi-translations)
Change of activity type
Topic shift
Puns, language play, shift of "key"
Topicalisation, topic/comment structure

Auer expresses doubts as to whether such lists of triggers provide a comprehensive explanation of code-switching, and with good reason. First, the triggers are not all the same sort of creature; some of them seem to be possible results of code-switching, rather than causes of it (e.g. perceived emphasis may follow from a switch rather than prompting it). Auer is also disturbed by the lack of reference to hierarchization of participant codes. Extrapolating from this to Czech, we might ask, for instance, whether "change of participant constellation", which can act as a trigger for either SC->CC or CC->SC, should be put in the same table as "puns or language play", where the insertion of a SC form into a CC text will play an entirely different role from the insertion of a CC form into a SC text. Certain items on the list also seem tautological in the sense that they can turn into the tail that wags the dog: seeing a code switch, for example, we may look too strenuously for a pragmatic reason to motivate it.

There are places in the corpus where what look like code-switch triggers appear:

7.3a „Už **zejtra**? Víš, že jsem na to úplně zapomněl?"
„Ale platí to, doufám?"..
„Abych pravdu řek, moc se mi to nehodí. Nechceš to přehodit na jindy?"
„Ne. **Zítra** v osm. Budeš si muset ráno zajet pro ty doklady,"
' "**Tomorrow** (CC) — already? You know, I forgot all about it."
"But it's still OK with you, isn't it?"
"To tell the truth, it's not very convenient. Can't we put it off till another time?"
"No. **Tomorrow** (SC) at eight. You'll have to go get the documents tomorrow morning." '

In 7.3a, Jakub tries to wriggle out of going to register his name officially on his daughter's birth certificate. His girlfriend, Pavla, is insistent. The repeated word 'tomorrow' shows up the first time in its CC form, *zejtra*, then later in its SC form, *zítra*.

A more textual reason for a shift can be seen in 7.3b, where a mother lectures her daughter:

7.3b   —**Von** tam za mnou přijel jeden **známej**.
       —**Kterej**?
       —Toho neznáš.
       —Když mě někdo někam pozve, tak si tam nezvu **jiného**, ne?
       —**Já ho nezvala**. (Kohout)
       ' "**Some guy I know** (CC) came to meet me there."
       "**Who** (CC)?"
       "You don't know him."
       "When someone invites me somewhere, I don't invite **someone else** (SC) along."
       "**I didn't invite him** (CC)." '

The narrator's daughter has returned early from a trip without her boyfriend, and her mother is trying to figure out why. In her first turn, she responds in CC, the same variety as her daughter uses. In her second turn, she issues a piece of advice, and the only clearly marked form in the sentence is SC. We can read it as a role switch: the mother moves from confidante to advisor, prompting the use of SC, or it can be seen as a closely related "change in activity." (The daughter's continuation in CC could then be a signal that she rejects the change in status or focus of the conversation.)

7.3c   „Vypadá to, že zase budu muset točit něco o našem nejvyšším," sdělil jí.
       „To je snad dobře?"
       „**Radši** točím zvířata než lidi. **Velká** zvířata," upřesnil. „Ale ne zas tak **velká**.
       Ani tak **stará**. A už vůbec ne **taková, co** jsou **vybrána** k odstřelu." (Klíma)
       ' "It looks like I'll have to film something about our lord and master again," he informed her.
       "Is that a good thing?"
       "I **prefer** (CC) filming animals to people. **Big** (SC) animals," he clarified. "But not quite that **big** (SC). Or that **old** (SC). And absolutely not **the kind** (SC) **that** (CC) are **chosen** (SC) to be shot." '

In 7.3c, the character Pavel's intent in choosing the formal neuter plural nominative accusative case ending is probably meant to be joking or ironic.

However, in some places we cannot necessarily find any motivation for these switches. Notable here is the presence of the CC relative pronoun *co* in 7.3c where we might have expected SC *která*. This is not a particularly unusual mixture in Czech, but it is difficult to explain in terms of code-switching, as we would have to posit a virtually instantaneous "dip" from one code to another and back again. The amount of switching in 7.3d is even greater:

7.3d Ten herec měl tak nádherně **modré oči**, že si tu barvu budu pamatovat **celý** život. Té se asi říká nebeská modř. Proto musel hrát **kladnýho** hrdinu, s **takovýma** **očima** by nikdo nevěřil, že je **zlej**. (Procházková)
'That actor had such fantastically **blue eyes** (SC) that I'll remember the color my **whole** (SC) life. **It's** (SC) probably what's called heavenly blue. That's why he had to play the **good** (CC) guy; with **eyes like those** (SC) no one would believe he was **bad** (CC).'

In 7.3d it is hard to discern any structural or literary motivation for the switching. In summary, it appears that while communicative triggers are occasionally used in literary texts, they are not the only points at which CC discourse can give way to SC discourse, and they do not explain the sort of casually mixed discourse that seems to occur in 7.3c and 7.3d.

Studies of structural constraints on code-switching grew out of an effort to link code-switching with GB theory. These studies have gone in two directions. The first attempted to prove that code-switching respected syntactic units like the noun phrase and verb phrase; however, as Gardner-Chloros 1995 notes, numerous counterexamples have already been brought to bear on this point. Czech literary dialogue also offers numerous examples violating these syntactic constraints, a few of which are given in 7.3e-g.

7.3e Prosím tě, **koukala** jsem se na něj jako na **krásnej** přírodní **úkaz**. Víš, jako se **lidi obdivujou zasněženejm** horám nebo moři. (Procházková)
'Come on, I was **looking** (CC) at him like at a **handsome** (CC) natural **phenomenon** (SC). You know, the way **people** (CC) **admire** (SC-CC) **snow-capped** (CC) mountains or the sea.'

7.3f A tamhle, ve **výrobě** nitroglycerinu **mají** plně **automatizovaný** zařízení na mísení tekutiny, všechno na dálku **ovladatelný**, a víte, jak to **mísí**? Ručně, kopištěma! (Klíma)
'And **over there** (CC), in the nitroglycerine **plant** (SC), they **have** (SC) fully **automated** (CC) machinery for mixing liquids, everything on **remote** (CC) control, and know how they **mix** (SC) it? By hand, **with** (SC) **paddles** (CC)!'

7.3g — Naučil jsem se myslet každou vteřinu na to, co nesmím.
— Co třeba?
— Třebas mít **velký oči**. (Kohout)
' "I learned to think every second about what I must not do."
"Like what?"
"Like biting off more than I could chew (lit. having **big** (CC) **eyes** (SC))" '

Several sorts of violations of syntactic restraints are shown here. In 7.3e, *krásnej úkaz* 'handsome phenomenon' has a CC phonemic feature in the adjective, and a SC phonemic feature in the noun. Within the phrase *lidi obdivujou zasněženejm horám* 'people admire snowcapped mountains' the subject *lidi* has a CC morphological ending; the verb has a CC morphological ending and a SC phonemic feature at the beginning. In 7.3f the VP *mají plně automatizovaný zařízení* '(they) have fully automated machinery' has a morphologically SC verb form, with the adjective having a CC form. The example in 7.3g is even more striking, because the switch occurs between adjective (CC) and noun (SC). Examples 7.1a and 7.1c also have phrases where syntactic constraints are violated. Evidently if these syntactic constraints function, they are not immediately evident in literary texts, where authors frequently have recourse to mixed forms. In and of itself, mixing of CC and SC forms in close syntactic proximity causes no particular aesthetic difficulties for some authors.

A second direction of research into syntactic constraints on code-switching looked at similarities of syntactic structures between codes; researchers working on this approach have posited that code switches can only occur at junctures where syntactic structures are congruent in both codes. Because the two varieties examined here are syntactically very similar (see 7.1), differing primarily in their grammatical forms and lexicon, the constraint imposed is trivial for our concerns; it rules out virtually no contexts for CC-SC switching and is clearly aimed at situations where bilingual code-switching takes place.

While some code-switching factors have been shown to function in these texts, they are clearly insufficient to explain completely the variation in constructed texts like these. Since the notion of sharply separated codes interacting according to changing syntactic, pragmatic and textual conditions is inadequate, we should look for another account that does.

Two researchers have offered general directions that may be of use to us in this search. Auer offers the following guidance:

> I have tried to argue that between the grammar of code-alternation on the one hand, and its social meaning for the bilingual community at large on the other, there is a third domain that needs to be taken into account: that of the sequential embeddedness of code-alternation in conversation. This domain is relatively independent of the others. Its autonomy is given by the fact that the basic principles by which code-alternation is used in conversation as a meaningful semiotic resource can be stated independently of both the grammar and the macro-social context of code-alternation. (Auer 1995:132)

Auer sees changes in code as a more or less inevitable result of interaction when more than one code is available. As well as considering the meaning and setting of any individual switch, we have to treat alternations in code as part of the interlocutors' developing strategies for the conversation. There will thus exist settings where, as Auer points out, code-switching is "the unmarked choice." This is true of conversations among the at least basically educated, who are the characters of the novels in question. Gardner-Chloros 1995 also takes issue with prevailing models of language contact, although her assertions go further than Auer's:

> The use of the term code-switching implies a binary choice - that at any given moment speakers are either operating in one mode or in another, which is clearly distinguishable from the first. This is an oversimplification. The type of language mixing which occurs in a given setting depends on a number of factors including the relative prestige of the varieties in question and the extent to which they are considered separate identifiable languages.... I shall therefore show firstly that what has been called code-switching in fact merges into various other interlingual phenomena, and that drawing clear lines between these phenomena is an ideological,

rather than an objective linguistic, activity. Secondly, I will provide arguments as to why I do not believe that the two languages, varieties or codes which make up code-switching can be discretely categorised in all but the most exceptional cases. (70)

Gardner-Chloros presents evidence that motivations for code-switching do not result in a predictable and quantifiable pattern of codes being switched; and that individuals mix codes in differing degrees and intensities: "The analogy with monolingual style-shifting is clear, and the range available to play on is probably broader." (1995:83)

Further, in "unconstrained switching mode," speakers can show allegiance to one or another variety by making quick symbolic detours into it: the mode is maintained even in the presence of a monolingual speaker by adding frequent tags from the other variety. (1995:85) The notion of symbolic allegiance to a particular variety can be a fruitful one in considering the particular mixture of features in literary dialogue. It has particular resonance for the finding in 5.4 that "tag" words characteristic of non-standard Czech are by far the most frequent lexical features in these texts.

If canonical models of code-switching have proved only somewhat enlightening and relevant, Auer's model of a separate motivational/strategic component to code-switching and Gardner-Chloros's picture of merging varieties are useful models for literary dialogue.

## 7.4. An alternate account of phonological correspondences

Previous studies established a hierarchy for the use of CC phonemes based on their positions in the word. CC phonemes were most frequent in desinence-final position, next most frequent in desinence-initial position, and rarest in roots. The three texts used in this survey each have their own internal hierarchy, but none of the three hierarchies match with each other, as can be seen in chart 7.4.1.

**Chart 7.4.1. Morphophonemic influence on use of CC /ɛj/, /iː/**

| frequency | Procházková | Kohout | Klíma |
|---|---|---|---|
| higher | desinence-initial | desinence-final* | roots |
| | desinence-final | roots* | desinence-final** |
| lower | roots | desinence-initial* | desinence-initial** |

*widely spaced for CC /ɛj/ but indistinguishable for CC /iː/.
**no CC tokens of /ɛj/ attested for either position.

Here it will be prudent to look at what these three terms "root", "desinence-initial" and "desinence-final" mean. Kučera originally distinguished only between root and desinence

positions; Kravčišinová and Bednářová, and Gammelgaard following them, divided
desinential positions further into final and non-final. At this level of division, the sets of
actual morphemes are quite limited in number, and are found exclusively in adjectival
declensions, as can be seen in chart 7.4.2.

**Chart 7.4.2. Long vowels in SC and CC desinences**

---

**Example: /dobr-/ 'good'**
SC /-i:/ vs. CC /-ɛj/:
    /dobri:/ vs. /dobrɛj/:  masculine nominative/accusative singular
SC /-i:C/ vs. CC /-ɛjC/:
    /dobri:x/ vs. /dobrɛjx/ genitive plural, all genders
    /dobri:m/ vs. /dobrejm/ dative plural, all genders
    /dobri:mɪ/ vs. /dobrejma/ instrumental plural, all genders
SC /-ɛ:/ vs. CC /-i:/:
    /dobrɛ:/ vs. /dobri:/ neuter nominative/accusative singular
    /dobrɛ:/ vs. /dobri:/ masculine inanimate/feminine nominative plural; all
    masculine/feminine accusative plural.
    /dobrɛ:/ vs. /dobri:/ feminine dative/genitive/locative singular
SC /-ɛ:C/ vs. CC /-i:C/:
    /dobrɛ:fio/ vs. /dobri:fio/ masculine/neuter genitive singular (+ animate accusative)
    /dobrɛ:mu/ vs. /dobri:mu/ masculine/neuter dative singular
    /dobrɛ:m/ vs. /dobri:m/ masculine/neuter locative singular

---

    As mentioned earlier, the phonemic features differentiating CC from SC can be
interpreted as features belonging either to the morphology or the lexicon of Czech. It will be
instructive to try reorganizing the data in this way.

    In 5.1, I pointed out that the long vowel alternations typical of the CC–SC divide are
found either root-internally or in adjectival desinences.  If we allow the root-internal
alternations to be a property of individual lexemes, as could follow from the analysis of
Hronek and other scholars in 3.6, then the primary difference between, say, "final desinence"
forms and "non-final desinence" forms is actually a matter of morphology: certain morphs
are more likely to appear in SC form than CC form, and vice-versa.

    The information in chart 7.4.3 is not nearly as neatly packaged as with a phonological
interpretation, but if we allow for the skewing of data that can occur with relatively low-
frequency features (marked in the table with an asterisk), the results look substantially the
same. Each phonological feature can be reconstructed from its "constituent" morphological
features, which occur within a narrow band of variation.  We can conclude that while a
morphological analysis may not in and of itself provide superior information to a
phonological analysis, it at least presents substantially the same information.

**Chart 7.4.3. Phonemes reinterpreted as morphemes**

|         | Procházková | Kohout | Klíma |
|---------|-------------|--------|-------|
| 100%    | m./n. dat. sg. 100* | -- | -- |
| 90-99%  | -- | -- | -- |
| 80-89%  | *gen. pl. 87.5\** <br> m./n. gen. sg. 84.2 <br> m./n. loc. sg. 83.3 <br> f. loc. sg. 83.3 <br> *dat. pl. 80.0\** | -- | -- |
| 70-79%  | f. obl. sg. 78.6 <br> m./f. nom. pl. 77.9 <br> *gen./loc. pl. 77.8\** <br> f. dat. sg. 75.0* <br> f. gen. sg. 75.0 | -- | -- |
| 60-69%  | n. nom. sg. 69.2 <br> *instr. pl. -ma 66.7\** | -- | -- |
| 50-59%  | *instr. pl. 50.0\** | f. sg. dat. 50.0* | -- |
| 40-49%  | -- | m./n. gen. sg. 45.9 <br> n. nom. sg. 42.0 | -- |
| 30-39%  | -- | m./f. nom. pl. 39.1 <br> m./n. loc. sg. 31.6 | -- |
| 20-29%  | -- | f. sg. gen. 28.6 <br> f. obl. sg. 27.7 <br> f. sg. loc. 20.0 <br> *loc. pl. 20.0\** | -- |
| 10-19%  | -- | *loc./gen. pl. 14.3* <br> *gen. pl. 12.5* | f. dat. sg. 16.7* |
| 1-9%    | -- | -- | f. loc. sg. 7.1 <br> m./n. gen. sg. 6.0 <br> f. obl. sg. 5.9 <br> m./f. nom. pl. 5.8 <br> n. nom. sg. 5.0 |
| 0%      | *loc. pl. 0.0\** <br> *instr. pl. -mi 0.0\** | m./n. dat. sg. 0.0* <br> *dat. pl. 0.0* | f. gen. sg. 0.0 <br> *gen/loc. pl. 0.0* <br> m./n. loc. sg. 0.0* <br> m./n. dat. sg. 0.0* <br> *dat. pl. 0.0\** |

plain text for CC /iː/ = SC /ɛː/; *italics for CC /ɛj/ = SC /iː/*; * = less than ten tokens overall
(numbers for masculine genitive singular includes the animate accusative singular)

One persistent feature that emerges from chart 7.4.3 is the unpredictability of infrequent and less frequent forms. There are three possible reasons for this unpredictability. First, it could be a statistical anomaly. Second, it could be a further problem connected with the low frequency of the form: the weight of examples connected with particular ordinary and yet infrequent contexts will be proportionally greater. Third, authors may, consciously or unconsciously, treat these infrequent forms differently from the more frequent forms.

Although the data from chart 7.4.3 do not provide any overwhelming evidence for distinguishing individual adjectival case morphemes from each other, there does seem to be a clear rationale for distinguishing a category of "adjectival desinence morphemes" from a category composed primarily of individual word roots. Here we might stop to consider Sgall and Hronek's assertion that while the appearance of CC phonemes in roots is highly idiosyncratic (see 3.6), its appearance in adjectival declensions is considerably more stable. If this is the case, then our second category — word roots — will be quite variable depending on the particular words that appear in the sample and their frequency. This interpretation essentially breaks the phonological correspondences into two batches: morphological and lexical.

Given the poor attestation of the other two phonemic alternations, /o/–/vo/ and /u:/–/ou/, it will not be possible to test any hypotheses regarding their usage in these texts. However, it is worth noting that a substantial number of attestations for the alternation /o/–/vo/ comes from only a few words: two common prepositions (*o* 'about, by' and *od* 'from') and one less common preposition (*ob* 'around'), as well as personal pronouns *(v)on* 'he, it', *(v)ona* 'she, it', *(v)ono* 'it' and *(v)oni, ona, ony* 'they'.[84] The proportion of forms in *(v)o-* consisting of the seven aforementioned words is shown in chart 7.4.4.

**Chart 7.4.4. Common words with initial /(v)o/**

| Word | Procházková | Kohout | Klíma |
|---|---|---|---|
| *o* 'about, against, around' | 35 | 37 | 63 |
| *od* 'from' | 16 | 19 | 12 |
| *on, ona, ono, oni, ony* 'third-person pronouns' | 20 | 16 | 34 |
| *vo* 'about, against, around' | - | 3 | - |
| *vod* 'from' | - | 3 | - |
| *von, vona, vono, voni* 'third-person pronouns' | - | 27 | - |
| **subtotal for these words** | **71** | **105** | **99** |
| total all words in (v)o- | 185 | 280 | 289 |
| **subtotal as percentage of total** | **38.4%** | **37.5%** | **34.3%** |

---

[84]  *ony* 'they (masculine inanimate and feminine)' and *ona* 'they (neuter)' do not have CC equivalents distinguishing animacy and gender. Their CC equivalent is *voni* 'they (all genders)'.

If we follow Townsend 1990 (36-38), who states that the use of prothetic /v/ is highly lexicalized, then the individual behavior of these words would have a strong impact on the choice of variants.[85] It may be, however, that the valuation attached to the CC form is so low that it is beyond consideration for most literary texts.

This generalization would also hold for the alternation /u:/–/ou/, if anything even more so than for /o/–/vo/. The environment yielding /u:/–/ou/ appears in only a few word roots (*úzký* 'narrow' and words derived from it, *úl* 'beehive' and so forth) and in nouns and adjectives with the lengthened version of the prefix *u-* (examples are *úřad* 'office', *účinný* 'effective', *útrata* 'loss'). Townsend (1990:34-36) found this feature to be more strongly lexicalized than /o/–/vo/, with only a small number of words, predominantly those from a rural context, where /ou/ lacked some additional stylistic or textual function.

Other CC phonetic/phonemic forms (consonant cluster simplifications and differences in vowel length) are rarely represented in these texts, as we saw in 5.1. Although CC does tend to have simplified consonant clusters where SC has complex ones, to have short or semi-short vowels in some places where SC has long ones, and to have long or semi-long vowels in certain emotive words where SC has a short vowel, these differences are predictable at most across small numbers of words. For example, according to the SSJČ there are seven words where initial SC /vʒd/ could correspond to CC /d/. These are *vždy, vždycky, vždycinky* 'always', *vždyť* 'after all', *vždyzelen, vždyzelený* 'evergreen (n., adj.)' *vždyživý* 'perennial' — a small number to begin with. If we posit that the last three are unlikely to have CC variants, and that the first is a strictly SC form, we are left with only three words having both SC and CC variants (*vždycky, vždycinky, vždyť*). Vowel length correspondences are even more unpredictable. Simple consonant clusters and occasional differences in vowel length are sporadically realized tendencies in CC as it relates to SC, and these differences are best captured as lexical, not phonological, ones.

## 7.5. Developing a scale-based model

Along the way, I have consistently been advocating that what is needed is a more flexible approach to the notion of what the two varieties of Czech are, and a way for them to interact that matches what we see in the texts under consideration. To develop a sliding scale like the one mentioned at the beginning of this chapter, I decided to define the features in terms of *officiality* and *unofficiality*, allowing for degrees and shadings, rather than with words like *standard* vs. *common*, which, not being opposites, suggests a category membership approach ("marked for SC–unmarked for CC" or "marked for CC–unmarked for SC").

This decision follows observations by several Czech scholars, and is succinctly expressed by Chloupek:

> The dichotomy of formal-informal has already changed its function. In addressing the public, i.e. o f f i c i a l communication, even semi-official, the formal language

---

85  Also possibly worth considering is the value attached to the common prefixes *o-, od-, ob-*, although here it could be argued that in many common words (especially nouns) the prefix is no longer perceived as a separate entity, which would cause problems for quantitative analysis.

serves, and, on the other hand, the informal serves the c o n f i d e n t i a l , the intimate; the former is important to the community, the latter is a matter of the personal. Under favourable conditions the formal language comes to be used for the welfare of the community, it becomes planned, institutionalized. The new contradiction is already less sharp: the signal for the changeover is the "casual language" becoming specialized and already showing stylistic features. The greater part of the population is of necessity diglossal and is beginning intentionally to select, to varying degrees and according to the type of utterance, means of expression within the scale of the official – intimate from the bookish to the folk-speech (and vulgar). (1987:97).

As suggested before, I will argue for a five-part cline within written Czech that encompasses the range of usage found in this corpus:

*Official written.* Traditionally assigned to SC. Not appropriate for depictions of informal styles of speech. Can give the impression of formality, and potentially of coldness or stuffiness, in speech.

*Neutral.* Traditionally assigned to SC or ColC, or no assignment made at all. Has a wide range of applicability, possibly fading out at the extremes of the spectrum (i.e inappropriate for highest or lowest registers). Includes some features that have strictly SC or CC variants, but also features that have no SC–CC opposition (not listed in the chart below).

*Unmarked unofficial.* Traditionally assigned to ColC or to CC. Is widely, although not universally, used for depicting speech. Its use outside depictions of speech is marked.

*Marked unofficial.* Traditionally assigned to CC, or rarely to ColC. Acceptable for depicting speech, but frequency of employment varies, indicating a lack of stylistic neutrality.

*Highly unofficial.* Traditionally assigned to CC. Rarely reflected in written dialogue, regardless of frequency in speech. Written form creates an immediate impression of non-standardness, possibly negative impressions for some readers. (These features may not make this impression at all in actual speech.)

This cline will suffice for the texts considered in this study. I suggested earlier that we needed to consider at least three types of unofficial language, which I have done here. I have rather crudely subdivided everything else into two categories (*official written* and *neutral*); it is not only possible but probable that studies focusing on standard narrative and non-fiction texts would subdivide those further. Emotive and temporal attributes could presumably also be considered, although I have not done so here.

The features discussed in chapters 5 to 7 can be arrayed on this cline based on both their description in grammars and handbooks and their appearance and use in this corpus. While the corpus usage will be decisive, reference to generally accepted norms is necessary as well to help interpret information from the corpus. Three assumptions thus underlie the classification in chart 7.5.1.

First, I incorporate a large number of commonly-held, relatively uncontroversial value judgments about variants as givens. This may include judgments proposed by Sgall, Hronek, Čermák, Townsend and others, such as "item *a* is felt to be quite informal" or "item *b* has a highly literary character." It certainly includes wider societal value judgments such as "item *c* is CC" and "item *d* is SC." At the same time, I use these judgments merely to indicate direction on the register scale, i.e. that *a* and *c* are found in lower registers than *b* and *d*.

**Chart 7.5.1. Registers in Czech in literary dialogue**

| Register | Phonology | Morphology | Syntax | Lexicon |
|---|---|---|---|---|
| Official Written | D SC /ɛː/ <br> E SC /iː/ | 8SC mohu <br> 14SC říci <br> 6SC lidé <br> 12SC pracuji <br> 7SC mohou <br> 11SC pracují <br> 10SC pány <br> 4SC dobří hráči <br> 2SC bychom <br> 17SC vedeme <br> 9SC nesl <br> 13SC prosí <br> 3SC dobrá auta | -li <br> predicate instr. <br> no auxiliary drop | bookish, etc. <br> (plus words <br> unmarked in <br> dictionaries but <br> generally viewed <br> as formal or non- <br> spoken) |
| Neutral | F SC /#o/ <br> G SC /#uː/ <br> SC vowel length, <br> consonant clusters | 8CC můžu <br> 14CC říct <br> 6CC lidi <br> 12CC pracuju <br> 7CC můžou <br> 5SC dělají, sázejí <br> 15SC s dobrým <br> 1SC bych <br> 16SC sázejí | anaphoric ellipsis <br> predicate nom. <br> relative *který* <br> unreduplicated <br> subjects | colloquial <br> ordinary <br> (plus many <br> words unmarked <br> in dictionaries) |
| Unmarked Unofficial | D1 CC /-iː/ <br> D2 CC /-iːC/ | 3CC dobrý auta <br> 10CC pánama <br> 17CC vedem <br> 11CC pracujou <br> 4SC dobrý hráči | other ellipsis <br> dislocations <br> repetitions <br> relative *co* <br> auxiliary drop <br> perfect tense | common Czech |
| Marked Unofficial | D3 CC /-iː-/ <br> E CC /ɛj/ | 9CC nes <br> 13CC prosej <br> 5CC dělaj, sázej | anacoluthon <br> interruptions <br> reduplicated <br> subject pronoun | regional <br> dialectal |
| Highly Unofficial | F CC /#vo/ <br> G CC /#ou/ <br> CC vowel length, <br> consonant clusters | 2CC bysme <br> 16CC sází <br> 15CC s dobrym <br> 1CC bysem | repairs <br> unfinished <br> sentences | professional <br> slang (plus <br> "crossover" <br> slang words) |

Basic value judgments are thus the background against which the study is conducted. It is designed to complement, refine and reconsider these judgments, not to overturn them.

This approach is a necessary one. If items *c* and *d* appear in the same corpus and are reckoned to be variants of the same feature *E*, the corpus will not necessarily tell us which of them is in a higher register and which in a lower one. I derive this basic "directionality" from common usage and, occasionally, from the considered opinions of linguists.

Second, the three texts in the corpus are assumed to fall in the mainstream of written language, and the dialogue they contain is presumed, for the most part, not to be highly stylized or unconventional in the manner of underground literature (although see especially the discussion of Kohout above). I therefore have not devoted extensive space to considerations of how style or authorial purpose may influence usage.[86]

Third, the scheme in chart 7.5.1 may not have universal applicability in Czech, but should serve as a model for similar schemes for other sorts of texts.

Chart 7.5.1 is structured so as to capture a number of generalizations about the features discussed as they appeared in the texts of the corpus.

First, when the CC variant of a feature appears on the scale, then its SC counterpart also appears on the scale.

Second, there are restrictions on how the variants are assigned to registers. These restrictions reflect beliefs about the current state of Czech as set out above. SC forms will appear in the first two registers; CC forms will appear in the last four. Both can occupy the "neutral" register. However, "neutral" assumes that a form is predominant in all contexts, meaning that both variants of a form cannot be neutral. There is therefore no scope for both the SC and the CC form to occupy the same register. The SC form will always appear in a higher register than the CC form (see above).

Third, the more frequent a CC variant was, the closer its rating was to "neutral." The less frequent it was, the further its rating was from "neutral." CC variants go down the scale as they get further from neutral, never up. Notice that all the CC features listed as "neutral" are those accepted for use in certain kinds of SC. However, not all CC features codified for use in SC fall in the neutral register. Most noticeably, the CC variants of features 11 (*pracujou*) and 16 (*sází*) fall respectively into the "unmarked unofficial" and "highly unofficial" registers.

Fourth, SC variants that appeared with high frequency received the designation "neutral." Those with lower frequency were designated "official written."

Fifth, where neither the SC variant nor the CC variant occupies the position "neutral," there was no predominant neutral variant.[87] In such instances, there is a "tug-of-war" between the two forms in the zone between them, which is indicated in my corpus by usage that varies from context to context, character to character, and text to text. SC forms will occupy the "official written" register, and CC forms will occupy one of the three "unofficial" registers. The further the CC form is down the scale, the more likely we are to find the SC form, even one designated "official written," in common use in literary dialogue. This range of influence for each variant thus spreads between different steps on the scale.

---

[86] Contrast this approach with Gammelgaard 1997, whose corpus of underground literature requires far more attention to the peculiarities of individual style.

[87] This echoes the discussion of Sgall et al. 1992 earlier in this work.

**Chart 7.5.2. Graphic representation of variant competition.**

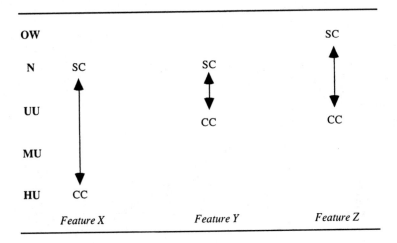

*Feature X*                    *Feature Y*                    *Feature Z*

Chart 7.5.2 shows graphically how this works. Given three different features — X, Y, and Z — which each have a "CC" and a "SC" variant, their occurrence in these texts is depicted by where those variants are placed on the cline. Feature X has a wide gap between the register of its CC variant and its SC one. In texts falling close to the "neutral" register, then, we will expect to see the SC variant realized almost exclusively. As the text's register moves closer to the "highly unofficial," we will expect to see the proportion of the CC variant increase. Features Y and Z have a CC feature with only a mild degree of unofficiality. The frequency of the CC form's occurrence will be largely be governed by the register of the SC form: in the case of feature Y, it will be less frequent, given the SC form's neutrality, while in the case of feature Z it will be more frequent, given the SC form's emphatic officiality.

Frequency is not the only determinant that led me to place variants in one or another slot. Especially in the realm of syntax, where data were sparse, I also considered the contexts in which features appeared and their apparent function in the texts. In addition, there are features mentioned in the analyses above that do not appear on the scale. For example, in the lexicon, certain sorts of slang and taboo words do not fit well into these categories. This fact shows again that dialogue in mainstream literary prose does not define all the possible registers of Czech.

I also propose that we can use a similar scale to classify texts as a whole, and not only features or variants of features. A text draws most consistently on the variants mentioned in its own basic register. Inconsistent usage arises at several points. First, when features are not explicitly mentioned in that register, then some amount of drawing from the registers immediately above and below is inevitable; this will result in features being realized inconsistently. Second, most literary texts will not fit neatly into a single slot on the scale, but rather will slide up or down the scale depending on the characters speaking and the situation. The position of texts with regards to the scale in chart 7.5.1 is shown in chart 7.5.3.

**Chart 7.5.3. Three texts and their register usage**

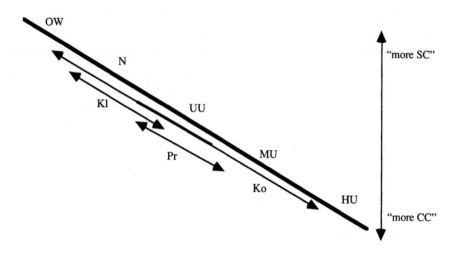

In chart 7.5.3, Klíma and Procházková are represented by lines stretching across one or two adjacent grades. Kohout, by contrast, has a much wider range of grades, depending on the character speaking and the situation, with the majority of speeches occurring near the middle of the band (the thickened portion of line). The designations "more SC" and "more CC" in the right margin indicate the relative proportion of forms marked as one or the other found in the texts; they are not intended to stand as labels for the texts themselves.

One generalization about Bohemian Czech that the scale in chart 7.5.1 captures nicely are the lacunae in the language's system of variety-neutral variants. This lack is mentioned in Chloupek 1987 and Sgall et al. 1992, although they are not the only scholars to discuss it. If there is any more universal validity to the scale, then those features missing an assignment in the "neutral" category and displaying the largest gap between their SC and CC variants will be precisely those where native speakers feel that a generally acceptable form is missing.

The feature assignments proposed in chart 7.5.1 can be compared to Čermák's 1987 suggestions on the acceptability of CC elements in written texts. There are numerous differences between the scale given above and Čermák's categories; nonetheless, there are also points of agreement.

Čermák assigns the vast majority of CC variants to his A rank, "accepted/normal in writing." This includes features realized only occasionally or at least far from consistently as CC in my corpus, including /ɛj/ for SC /iː/ and morphological features 3, 4, 10, 11 and 17, which figured in much lower spots on my scale. The phonological feature /#vo/ and morphological feature 9 receive acceptability rating A-B, which is somewhere between A and "sometimes accepted", or B. These also scored much lower in my corpus for frequency and were put further down the list. My counts agreed with Čermák's hypotheses on the high frequency of CC elements in morphological features 7, 8, 12 and 14, which are now codified for some or all SC. We also agreed on the surprisingly low acceptability of realization of morphological feature 13 as CC, on the negligible appearance in written Czech of CC /#ou/, and on the virtual unacceptability of common phonetic reductions like *pude* for *půjde* 'he goes', *dycky* for *vždycky* 'always' and *říkám* for *říkám* 'I say'.

As explanation for the differences, although Čermák lists personal correspondence and modern literature as the two places most likely for these elements to occur, it is not clear what aspect of modern literature he has in mind. Čermák also notes that his ratings are impressionistic rather than being based on data. (1987:140, 142). His evaluations are consistently more "liberal" in their permissiveness toward CC features than my data suggest.

We can also compare the scale above to Bílý's classification system (1999:90). We might expect that any variant Bílý classes as "normal in speech and writing" should prove an acceptable compromise that would be widely used in portraying literary dialogue (i.e. that should fit into my "neutral" category). In fact, many of the variants Bílý regards as neutral come out as marked as clearly "official" or "unofficial" on my scale, and many of the variants Bílý regards as "substandard" are widely attested in my corpus. The data from my survey suggest that many SC forms are not deemed neutral for portrayal of speech, whereas Bílý's judgments suggest the opposite should be true. Part of this is related to Bílý's use of the terms "normal," "elaborate" and "substandard," which are, in my opinion, too elastic to be useful to linguists and fail to mesh adequately with my own. It is fully conceivable that a writer might feel a particular variant to be substandard, for instance, and yet recognize that it is widely employed with no particular aesthetic function; conversely, a writer might regard a different variant as "normal" and yet eschew it for one he feels to be "excessively elaborate" because that is the way he believes a particular character will speak. Bílý's classification scheme is best approached strictly the way he intended it — as a guide to his own authorial judgment that does not claim to predict how others write or what will actually be found in literary works.

## 7.6. Final excursus on Colloquial Czech

Regardless of what conclusions we reach about the status of CC and SC as separate codes, the idea of a "colloquial Czech" layer used for "standard conversations" and containing a prescribed mixture of certain CC and SC forms, finds some support in my data, but not enough to establish it convincingly as a discrete linguistic variety. Certain morphological features classed as ColC do appear in these text, and are amply attested. However, other features excluded from ColC are also well-documented, making it difficult to argue for any grouping of these ColC features as a natural class. The lexicon in two texts — Procházková's and Kohout's — is certainly generously sprinkled with items "inadmissible" in any strict definition of ColC. It seems unlikely to me that novelistic dialogue can be classed as ColC unless we are to broaden the definition of ColC substantially and let it draw on a much wider morphological and lexical base. Under most criteria only Klíma's dialogue could be convincingly seen as ColC.

It could be argued that novelistic dialogue is an eminently logical place to expect ColC, straddling as it does the boundaries between private and public discourse, and that the absence of ColC in these works therefore clearly proves its nonexistence. The reality is probably more ambiguous. The absence of ColC in a place well-suited to it is not proof of its nonexistence, but does remove one more clear place where ColC "should" be used. The fact that Klíma's dialogue is, in many respects, representative of aspects of ColC does not establish anything more than a single possibility for realizing dialogue in literature. I will follow Hronek (1972:15) and others in suggesting that ColC, if we wish to name such a creature, is simply a particular admixture of variant forms, differentiated from SC and CC only by quantitative, not qualitative means; no codification of it as a separate variety or code seems possible. The alternative term *běžně mluvená čeština* 'ordinary spoken Czech' is probably more appropriate for the mixture of forms used in most conversation, as it does not imply a strictly defined language variety.

## 7.7. Reinterpreting the four "layers" of the interface

Despite the difficulties discussed above in typing and evaluating lexical items, the influence of individual lexical units is a recurring theme in this study. While previous studies have taken either phonemic variation (Gammelgaard, Hammer) or morphological variation (Sgall and Hronek) as the level on which the SC–CC opposition is realized in code-switching, I offer instead the clines of lexical items in 5.4 as the fundamental unit of organization. In nearly every way a cline offers a more satisfactory resolution than a code-switching model.

Even if we set the various descriptive problems aside, SC–CC phonemic distinctions have been shown to be riddled with lexical exceptions — items that are either highly accepting of CC phonology or that do not admit it. Furthermore, the best explanation for usage and aesthetic differences between SC and CC phonological variants in different word positions appears to be that a limited number of morphemes are involved in these differences. It may in the end be easiest to see the phonemic hierarchies discussed earlier as a historically grounded "shorthand" for a set of morphemic and lexical hierarchies. In this account, paired items like *mlýn–mlejn* 'mill' and *výmluva–vejmluva* 'excuse', where the alternation /i:/–/ej/ occurs in the stem, would be treated similarly to *dívka–holka* 'girl' and other "suppletive" lexical pairs explored in 5.4. Words with these "regular phonemic" alternations would represent significant subsets within the lexicon, but, as has been shown earlier, the functions of these variants are different enough from set to set that there may be less reason for treating them as a group than has previously been assumed. Paired items like *krásným–krásnejm* 'beautiful (dative plural)' and *krásné–krásný* 'beautiful (feminine genitive/dative/locative singular)', where the phonemic alternations /i:/–/ej/ and /e:/–/i:/ occur in the desinence, occur in only a few morphological contexts and could easily be treated under the rubric of morphology.

The occasional quasi-phonetic spelling that marks non-standard vowel length or simplified consonant clusters is best treated as a feature of natural speech production. Such spellings are found only irregularly in these texts. Each of them typically occurs in a very small number of lexemes, and the types of correspondences that show up (i.e. the particular vowels or consonants involved) are not regular or predictable across the phonemic inventory. It is therefore sensible to treat individual examples of quasi-phonetic spelling as lexicalized non-standard forms.

It is somewhat easier to define the morphological units that should participate in the SC–CC opposition, and there are far fewer restrictions on the use of these forms, but there is still a strong differentiation between the more widely applicable forms and other, more narrowly applicable ones. Morphological units might thus also be best seen as taking their place on a usage cline, rather than as participating in a binary alternation ("marked/not marked in speech" vs. "marked/not marked in writing"). We might even want to give this morphological hierarchy prominence over "root-based" alternations, due to its frequency and combinatory possibilities with lexical root alternations.

As we saw in 5.3, many features typically treated under the rubric of syntax can equally easily be treated as lexical or morphological phenomena, and are perhaps treated as syntax primarily for the purpose of "fleshing out" the SC-CC opposition and making it seem more fully realized at all levels. Those features that cannot be reanalyzed as lexical or morphological phenomena are often features of *impromptu speech vs. scripted speech*, rather than of *non-standard vs. standard speech*. We are still left with a number of syntactic characteristics that seem to distinguish CC forms from SC forms, but again the functions of these forms vary, and a cline is again a more appropriate model than a bifurcation.

When we come to evaluate the nature of these variants overall, it is therefore more fruitful to interpret the standard vs. non-standard distinction as a matter of individual units, both root-based ("lexical") and inflection-based ("morphological"), instead of as consistent phonemic, morphological and syntactic distinctions. The penetration of CC elements into literary texts indicates that authors are to varying extents abandoning a strict genre-based divide between CC and SC in favor of increasing the lexical and pragmatic expressive possibilities of their language. Hammer 1985 has shown that this process has already been realized in speech, with SC elements penetrating ordinary speech to a remarkable degree among the educated classes. As particular words, morphemes or phonemes develop additional meanings and connotations, the simple SC–CC divide grows less important in each instance.

Is there still any room for the terms "CC" and "SC" in this account? The answer is yes, although with a more limited role than we assumed at first.

First, I would designate SC and CC as *registers* utilizing particular sets of variants or sets of alternatives rather than as hard-and-fast *codes*. In a very real sense, marking a form as belonging to SC in this account simply means that it is the more official of two available forms, while marking it as CC means it is the more unofficial of two available forms. The use of these forms in different registers and different situations is a matter of negotiation based on the degree of (in)formality of both variants.

Second, there are plenty of texts and discourse situations that exist at either end of the spectrum, which are characterized by a consistent adherence to one or the other set of variants. These can be convincingly identified as "SC" or "CC"; we could call them prototypical examples of these varieties. Still, the existence of literature, journalism, and ordinary educated conversations containing some mixture of forms militates against delineating sharp boundaries between the two varieties.

Third, the terms "SC" and "CC" are a convenient shorthand among speakers and in texts that serve a codifying function, such as grammars and dictionaries. They constitute a recommended usage which is imprecise enough to give the user some scope for individual judgment — perhaps enough to indicate appropriateness or inappropriateness in a given situation. Hammer's data give a fascinating clue of this sort, which is reproduced in Sgall and Hronek 1992 and elsewhere. In one of Hammer's taped conversations, an interlocutor began by describing her job. She was soon interrupted by someone saying *a už mluví spisovně!*, literally 'and she's talking standard already!' The second speaker's comment was not intended to describe the language variety, but to draw attention to the absurdity of the numerous SC forms in what was supposed to be an informal setting.

Finally, the notion of a "standard Czech" versus a "common" one is also a cultural artifact, born of 200 years of careful linguistic preservation and the cultivation of archaic words, forms, and constructions in the language. The rationale for the existence of SC and CC as terms may have less to do with their usage in any given situation and more to do with a global view of the language as a divided one; individual Czechs' evaluations of particular forms, and their usage of them, may not always match with scholarly definitions of SC and CC as a whole.[88] This cultural aspect is perhaps the remnant of an earlier period in which true diglossia was evident or strict code-switching took place (see chapter 8). Paradoxically, it may be this "heritage" aspect of SC that is the best rationale for its continued existence and the most appropriate way to recognize its contributions to the diversity of modern Czech.

---

[88] I wish to thank Petr Sgall for emphasizing to me the cultural and social dimensions of SC and CC for a definition of language variation.

# 8. Conclusions

It remains to take a second look at the status of Czech diglossia in Bohemia and, having come to some conclusions regarding its position, to reexamine what studies of code-switching and bilingual behavior can bring to our discussion of the Czech language situation, and what that situation contributes to the picture of language varieties more globally.

In this analysis, we have reduced the linguistic component of Czech "diglossia" to a collection of lexical and morphological items arrayed on a cline primarily indicating register. In such an account, Czech in Bohemia begins to look more like a conventional West European language, although it continues to have a far richer range of alternative forms than does English, for instance. In this respect, Czech still stands out, even when compared to closely related and similarly morphologically rich languages like Polish and Russian.

This does not necessarily mean that diglossia as such never existed in the Czech lands, or that Havránek's quasi-diglossic pronouncements of mid-century were incorrect. As Ferguson notes:

> Diglossia is likely to come into being when the following three conditions hold in a speech community: (1) There is a sizable body of literature in a language closely related to (or even identical with) the natural language of the community, and this literature embodies, whether as source (e.g. divine revelation) or reinforcement, some of the fundamental values of the community. (2) Literacy in the community is limited to a small elite. (3) A suitable period of time, of the order of several centuries, passes from the establishment of (1) and (2). (1959:247):

The first two of these conditions were certainly present in the Czech lands in the late eighteenth and early nineteenth centuries, from whence we date the establishment of a separate, archaizing standard code. As far as the current situation, in many respects, the Czech lands look to be a textbook case of the retreat of diglossia, which, Ferguson posits, occurs under certain circumstances:

> These include trends toward (1) more widespread literacy (whether for economic, ideological or other reasons), (2) broader communication among different regional and social segments of the community (e.g. for economic, administrative, military or ideological reasons), (3) desire for a full-fledged 'national' language as an attribute of autonomy or sovereignty. (1959:247).

Again, the Czech-speaking territories have certainly seen massive social mobility (both up and down the scale) and advances in literacy, the former due in part to the massive dislocations and changes that followed independence in 1918, the Communist coup of 1948, and the Velvet Revolution of 1989.

In both the formation and dismantling of diglossia, however, the Czechs lack one potentially important condition. For the formational conditions, diglossia was never as fully rooted in the Czech lands as elsewhere, given its relatively short heyday (probably less than a hundred years from its firm establishment on Czech soil to the beginning of its demise). In the dismantling phase, too, there is a catch: all indications are that Czechs regard SC as precisely that "full-fledged national language" Ferguson refers to. Ferguson's statement seems more applicable to supernational standards like Arabic, German and French; it seems unlikely that a standard language based on CC would have more of a national character than SC has in the eyes of the ordinary populace.[89] This inherent high regard for SC would curb any tendencies to rid contemporary Czech altogether of its SC elements. Indeed, the fact that SC elements occur within CC texts and vice versa indicates that the language has already coopted its diglossic markers for use as register and discourse markers.

The notion that sharp boundaries exist between SC and CC has thus been gradually effaced, with the two varieties' essential separateness giving way in places to more discourse-oriented mixing to show foregrounding and backgrounding, rather than to mark situation. These trends are especially notable at "contact points" in the language where drawing on both varieties is not only possible but in many respects has come to constitute the norm.

The speech of ordinary educated Czechs, in both private and public space, is one such point, as has been shown in Hammer 1985 and in Kravčišinová and Bednářová 1968. Anecdotal evidence suggests that oral art forms, such as popular music, radio, television and theater, are also contact points of this sort, although no studies have as of yet been done that bear this out.

The situation in predominantly written texts is more complex. Gammelgaard 1997 has demonstrated that if a consistent mix of SC and non-SC forms is adopted in a text, the same foregrounding and backgrounding elements characteristic of speech can be brought out. Short 1992 discusses a number of examples from a popular novel that suggest distinct stylistic and literary agendas which can be pursued by mixing SC and CC items. Since the sort of narrative used in these two studies is still an "alternative" tradition, it is not yet clear that it will provide a model for literary texts in general. However, the current study suggests that this mixing of varieties to produce foregrounding and backgrounding effects may already be so deeply anchored in speech that it must be reflected to some extent in literature if literary dialogue is to have any degree of verisimilitude. In this account, dialogue in literature is, along with popular journalism, one of the "bridges" by which non-SC elements enter texts traditionally reserved for SC.

Certainly in this large and growing stratum of oral and written texts that draw both on SC and CC, we can see ample evidence of a fusion of the two varieties. The fact that the literary dialogue surveyed in this study falls broadly in line with many of the trends observed for other literary texts and for certain sorts of speech argues that what we are seeing is not exceptional examples of "intellectual posing" or literary conceit confined to certain unusual sorts of texts. Instead, it is a wider shift within Czech that is being implemented both in the spoken and the written language, albeit in somewhat different ways.

---

[89] Even if we were to regard Czech as a 'multinational' language spoken by Bohemians, Moravians and Silesians, it would still be hard to see the appeal of a separate Bohemian language. Bohemians, as the majority population of Czech speakers, are not noted for their local patriotism or any strong sense of Bohemian identity differentiating them from Moravians and Silesians; any sense of national identity is bound up in being Czechs. Indeed, the language is hardly conducive to such nationalism; the Czech words *Čech, český*, are commonly used to mean both 'Bohemian' and 'Czech'.

Viewed from a comparative perspective, the Czech language situation underscores the importance of distinguishing *intralinguistic* diglossia and *interlinguistic* diglossia. While the parallels between the two types of diglossia are evident, the Czech language situation in Bohemia, like other single-language diglossic systems, is largely a product of internal developments; as Daltas notes, it is a fundamentally different creature from bilingual diglossia:

> Indeed, there remains the fact that Fishmanian diglossia classifies together (a) settings of societal bilingualism in which, as a result of colonialism, immigration or the formation of multinational states, a foreign language serves the H function and a local variety the L functions; and (b) monolingual societies whose high degree of societal compartmentalization has led to a significant formal and functional diversification of the same language leading to two varieties, one of them serving H and the other L functions. (1994:347)

As he points out, the former is a prosperous group, common in the modern world and easily developed over a short time span; the latter, because of its long gestational period, is rarer and "far more likely to fall victim to the modern way of life that, as Fishman (1980:12) notes, constantly undermines societal compartmentalization in the interests of efficiency and internationalism."

If these distinctions are kept in mind, Czech is representative (if only partially so) of a much smaller set of languages whose compartmentalization developed slowly, over generations, and whose gradual evolution away from compartmentalization is fundamentally different from the evolutionary processes that take place in societal bilingualism. Bohemian Czech may therefore provide an excellent example of a diglossic language situation that is resolving into a type of register stratification more or less typical of European languages, albeit one marked by more pervasive distinctions marking these registers than are found in most languages. The erosion of the traditional situationally-based distinctions between variant forms in Czech, coupled with the realization that the differences between SC and CC are less systematic than is generally believed, means that the various features that used to characterize one variety or the other are being constantly reevaluated, forming in the end a more graduated scale of acceptability. At the same time, it gradually removes the incentive for viewing Bohemian Czech as two completely separate entities comprising a single language system.

# BIBLIOGRAPHY

Atkinson, Dwight and Douglas Biber. 1994. Register: A Review of Empirical Research. In Biber and Finegan, eds., 351-385.

Auer, Peter. 1995. The Pragmatics of Code-Switching: A Sequential Approach. In Milroy and Muysken,eds., 115-135.

Auty, Robert. 1976. Problems of the Formation and Development of the Czech Literary Language. In Magner, ed., 82-88.

Bartošek, Jaroslav. 1997. Diskutovat, ale ne pořád. *Jazykovědné aktuality* 34:44-51.

Bělič, Jaromír, et al. 1962. Problematika obecné češtiny a jejího poměru k jazyku spisovnému. *Slovo a slovesnost* 23 (2):108-126.

Bermel, Neil. 1997. Examining Dialogue in Czech Literary Texts. *Czech Language News* 8:6-8.

Biber, Douglas. 1988. *Variation Across Speech and Writing.* Cambridge: Cambridge University Press.

Biber, Douglas and Edward Finegan, eds. 1994. *Sociolinguistic Perspectives on Register.* New York and Oxford: Oxford University Press.

Bílý, Milan. 1999. Linguists Go Home! Or: Hands off the Riches of the Czech Language! *Scando-Slavica* 45:81-94.

Blom, Jan-Petter, and John Gumperz. 1972. Social Meaning in Linguistic Structure: Code-Switching in Norway. In Gumperz and Hymes, eds., 407-434.

Čermák, František. 1987. Relations of Spoken and Written Czech. *Wiener Slawistischer Almanach* 20:133-150.

———. 1993. Spoken Czech. In Eckert, ed., 27-41.

———. 1997. Obecná čeština: je součástí české diglosie? *Jazykovědné aktuality* 34:34-43.

Čermák, František and Petr Sgall. 1997. Výzkum mluvené češtiny: jeho situace a potřeby. *Slovo a slovesnost* 58:15-25.

Čmejrková, Světla. 1997. Čeština v síti: psanost či mluvenost? (O stylu e-mailového dialogu.) *Naše řeč* 80:225-247.

Čmejrková, Světla and František Štícha, eds. 1994. *The Syntax of Sentence and Text. Linguistic and Literary Studies in Eastern Europe* 42. Amsterdam and Philadelphia: John Benjamins.

Čmejrková, Světla et al., eds. 1994. *Writing vs. Speaking: Language, Text, Discourse, Communication. Tübinger Beiträge zur Linguistik* 392. Tübingen: Gunter Narr Verlag.

———. 1998. *Dialoganalyse VI: Referate der 6. Arbeitstagung, Prag 1996.* Tübingen: Max Niemeyer.

Chloupek, Jan. 1987. The Changing Dichotomy Between Informal and Formal Utterance. In Chloupek et al., eds., 94-105.

Chloupek, Jan et al., eds. 1987. *Reader in Czech Sociolinguistics.* Amsterdam and Philadelphia: John Benjamins.

Cochran, Effie Papatzikou. 1997. An Instance of Triglossia? Codeswitching as Evidence for the Present State of Greece's "Language Question." *International Journal of the Sociology of Language* 126:33-62.

Cummins, George. 1994. Intercodal Collision in Narrative: Spoken and Written Language in Literary Narrative. In Čmejrková et al., eds., 361-366.

Daltas, Periklis. 1994. The Concept of Diglossia from Ferguson to Fishman to Fasold. In *Themes in Greek Linguistics*, ed. Irene Philippaki-Warburton et al., 341-348. Amsterdam: John Benjamins.

Daneš, František. 1957. Americká studie o mluvené češtině. *Naše řeč* 40:296-300.

──────. 1979. Postoje a hodnoticí kritéria při kodifikaci. In ÚJČ, ed., 79-91.

──────. 1987. Values and Attitudes in Language Standardization. In Chloupek et al., eds., 204-245.

──────. 1994. Feedback Dynamics Between Written and Spoken. In Čmejrková et al., eds., 47-54.

Dankovičová, Jana. 1999. Czech. In *Handbook of the International Phonetic Association: A Guide to the Use of the IPA*, 70-73. Cambridge: Cambridge University Press.

Davidová, Dana et al. 1997. *Mluvená čeština na Moravě*. Acta Facultatis Philosophicae Universitatis Ostravensis 106. Ostrava: Philosophical Faculty of Ostrava University.

Dickins, Tom. 1994. Linguistic Varieties in Czech: Problems of the Spoken Language. *Slavonica* 1:20-46.

Dil, Afia. 1986. Diglossia in Bangla: A Study of Shifts in the Verbal Repertoire of the Educated Classes in Dhaka, Bangladesh. In Fishman, et al., eds., 451-465.

Eckert, Eva. 1993. Introduction. In Eckert, ed., 3-26.

Eckert, Eva, ed. 1993. *Varieties of Czech: Studies in Czech Sociolinguistics*. Atlanta: Rodopi.

Ferguson, Charles A. 1994. Dialect, Register and Genre: Working Assumptions about Conventionalization. In Biber and Finegan, eds., 15-30.

──────. 1959 (1972). Diglossia. *Word* 15:325-340. Reprinted in *Language and Social Context*, ed. Pier Paolo Giglioli, 232-251. London: Penguin.

Filipec, Josef. 1979. Kodifikace a slovník. In ÚJČ, eds., 190-197.

Fishman, Joshua. 1972. Domains between Micro- and Macrosociolinguistics. In Gumperz and Hymes, eds., 435-453.

──────. 1980. Bilingualism and Biculturism as Individual and as Societal Phenomena. *Journal of Multilingual and Multicultural Development* 1 (1):3-15.

Fishman, Joshua, et al., eds. 1986. *The Fergusonian Impact. Volume 2: Sociolinguistics and the Sociology of Language*. Berlin: Mouton de Gruyter.

Francescato, Guiseppe. 1986. Bilingualism and Diglossia in their Mutual Relationship. In Fishman, et al., eds., 395-401.

Gammelgaard, Karen. 1996. Dobrovský's Czech Standard Language Norm. In Gammelgaard, Karen. *Two Studies on Written Language*, 22-36. *Meddelelser* 74. Oslo: Universitet i Oslo Slavisk-baltisk avdeling.

──────. 1997. *Spoken Czech in Literature*. Acta Humaniora 18. Oslo: Scandinavian University Press.

──────. 1999. Common Czech in Czech Linguistics. *Slavonica* 5 (2):32-51.

Gardner-Chloros, Penelope. 1995. Code-Switching in Community, Regional and National Repertoires: The Myth of the Discreteness of Linguistic Systems. In Milroy and Muysken, eds., 68-90.

Garvin, Paul L. 1994. The Analysis of Spoken and Written Data in the Light of Language Data Processing. In Čmejrková et al., eds., 63-75.

Goldblatt, Harvey. 1984. The Language Question and the Emergence of Slavic National Languages. In Scaglione, Aldo, ed., 119-173.

Grygar-Rechziegel, Adela. 1990. On Czech Diglossia. In *Czech Studies: Literature, Language, Culture,* ed. Mojmír Grygar, 9-29. Amsterdam and Atlanta: Rodopi.

Gumperz, John and Dell Hymes, eds. 1972 (1986). *Directions in Sociolinguistics: The Ethnography of Communication.* Oxford: Basil Blackwell.

Hammer, Louise. 1985. *Prague Colloquial Czech: A Case Study in Code-Switching.* Ph.D. dissertation: Indiana University.

———. 1993. The Function of Code Switching in Prague Colloquial Czech. In Eckert, ed., 63-78.

Havránek, Bohuslav. 1932. Úkoly spisovného jazyka a jeho kultura. In Havránek and Weingart, eds., 32-84.

———. 1963. Na závěr dvouleté diskuse o obecné a hovorové češtině. *Slovo a slovesnost* 24:254-262.

Havránek, Bohuslav and Miloš Weingart, eds. 1932. *Spisovná čeština a jazyková kultura.* Prague: Melantrich.

Hlavsa, Zdeněk. 1994. Writing vs Speaking from a Prescriptive Point of View. In Čmejrková et al., eds., 397-401.

Hlavsová, Jaroslava. 1997. Čeština v České republice jako jazyk „nevlastní". *Slovo a slovesnost* 58:185-196.

Hronek, Jiří. 1972. *Obecná čeština.* Prague: Univerzita Karlova.

Hubáček, Jaroslav. 1979. O slangu z hlediska jazykové kultury. In ÚJČ, eds., 212-216.

Hudson, Alan. 1994. Diglossia as a Special Case of Register Variation. In Biber and Finegan, eds., 294-314.

Hudson, Richard. 1980. *Sociolinguistics.* Cambridge: Cambridge University Press.

Jacobson, Rodolfo, ed. 1990. *Codeswitching as a Worldwide Phenomenon.* Series XIII (Linguistics) vol. 11. New York: Peter Lang.

Jahr, Ernst Håkon and Karol Janicki. 1995. The Function of the Standard Variety: A Contrastive Study of Norwegian and Polish. *International Journal of the Sociology of Language* 115:25-45.

Jakobson, Roman. 1932. O dnešním brusičství českém. In Havránek and Weingart, eds., 85-122.

Jančáková, Jana et al., eds. 1995. *Spisovná čeština a jazyková kultura 1993: sborník z olomoucké konference.* Prague: Filozofická fakulta Univerzity Karlovy.

Jedlička, Alois. 1963. K problému normy a kodifikace spisovné češtiny (oblastní varianty v spisovné normě). *Slovo a slovesnost* 24 (1):9-20.

———. 1979. Teorie jazykové kultury dnes. In ÚJČ, eds., 12-20.

Jelínek, Milan. 1979. Posuny v stylistické charakteristice jazykových prostředků a jejich kodifikace. In ÚJČ, eds., 109-121.

Klíma, Ivan. 1993. *Čekání na tmu, čekání na světlo.* Prague: Český spisovatel.

Kohout, Pavel. 1993. *Sněžím.* Prague: Český spisovatel.

Kolářová, Ivana. 1996. Mluvenostní stylizace a využití nespisovných výrazů v některých prozaických dílech současné české literatury. In Šrámek, ed., 166-168.

Komárek, Karel. 1996. Charakterizační funkce spisovného jazyka v uměleckých textech. In Šramek, ed., 169-170.

Kořenský, Jan. 1997. O hodnotách pražského funkcionalismu, jazykové kultury a o češtině včera i dnes nekonvenčně. *Slovo a slovesnost* 58:35-42.

Kraus, Jiří. 1987. On the Sociolinguistic Aspects of the Notion of Functional Style. In Chloupek et al., eds., 83-93.

————. 1992. Proměny řečnického stylu v češtině. *Slovo a slovesnost* 53:1-9.

————. 1993. Does Spoken Literary Czech Exist? In Eckert, ed., 42-49.

Kraus, Jiří et al. 1981. Současný stav a vývojové perspektivy kodifikace spisovné češtiny. *Slovo a slovesnost* 42:228-238.

Kravčišinová, K. and B. Bednářová. 1968. "Z výzkumu běžně mluvené češtiny." *Slavica Pragensia* 10:305-320.

Kučera, Henry. 1955. Phonemic Variations of Spoken Czech. *Word* 11 (4):575-602.

————. 1958. Inquiry into Coexistent Phonemic Systems in Slavic Languages. In *American Contributions to the Fourth International Congress of Slavicists, Moscow, September 1958*, 169-189. The Hague: Mouton.

————. 1961. *The Phonology of Czech*. The Hague: Mouton.

————. 1973. Language Variability, Rule Interdependency, and the Grammar of Czech. *Linguistic Inquiry* 4 (4):499-521.

————. 1980. The Language Dilemma of a Czech Writer. *World Literature Today* 54 (4):577-581.

Leška, Oldřich. 1994. Some Remarks on Semiotic Aspects of Written Language. In Čmejrková et al., eds., 403-406.

Linhartová, Věra. 1996. Dilema spisovnosti v literatuře. In Šrámek, ed., 172-175.

Mackey, William F. 1986. The Polyglossic Spectrum. In Fishman et al., eds., 237-243.

Magner, Thomas F., ed. 1976. *Slavic Linguistics and Language Teaching*. Columbus, OH: Slavica.

Masaryk University Czech Language Institute. 1995. *Příruční mluvnice češtiny*. Prague: Lidové Noviny.

Mathesius, Vilém. 1932. O požadavku stability ve spisovném jazyce. In Havránek and Weingart, eds., 14-31.

Michálková, Věra. 1979. Vývojový pohyb v české tvaroslovné kodifikaci. In ÚJČ, eds., 173-179.

Micklesen, Lew R. 1978. Czech Sociolinguistic Problems. *Folia Slavica* 1 (3):437-455.

Milroy, James and Lesley Milroy. 1999. *Authority in Language: Investigating Standard English. Third Edition*. London: Routledge.

Milroy, Lesley and Pieter Muysken, eds. 1995. *One Speaker, Two Languages: Cross-disciplinary Perspectives on Code-Switching*. Cambridge: Cambridge University Press.

Müllerová, Olga and Jana Hoffmannová. 1997. Čeština spisovná, hovorová, obecná... a hlavně mluvená (v současné komunikaci a v současném výzkumu). *Slovo a slovesnost* 58:42-54.

Müllerová, Olga et al., eds. 1992. *Mluvená čeština v autentických textech*. Prague: Nakladatelství H&H.

Nebeská, Iva. 1996. *Jazyk, norma, spisovnost*. Acta Universitatis Carolinae Philologica Monographia 126. Prague: Philosophical Faculty, Charles University.

Neščimenko, Galina. 1994. Dixotomii "monologičeskaja – dialogičeskaja reč'" i "pis'mennaja – ustnaja reč'" i ix značimost' dlja modelirovanija stroenija nacional'nogo jazyka. In Čmejrková et al., eds., 219-226.

Ouředník, Patrick. 1992. *Šmírbuch jazyka českého (2. vydání)*. Prague: Ivo Železný.

Palková, Zdena. 1994. Mluvená čeština ve veřejných projevech (k problematice řečových vzorů). In *Přednášky z XXXVI. běhu Letní školy slovanských studií*, ed. Jan Kuklík and Jiří Hasil, 67-82.. Prague: Univerzita Karlova.

Paolillo, John C. 1997. Sinhala Diglossia: Discrete or Continuous Variation? *Language in Society* 26:269-296.

PMČ – See entry under Masaryk University Czech Language Institute.

Procházková, Lenka. 1982 (1991). *Oční kapky*. Brno: Atlantis.

Scaglione, Aldo, ed. 1984. *The Emergence of National Languages*. Ravenna: Longo Editore.

Scotton, Carol Myers. 1986. Diglossia and Code Switching. In Fishman, et al., eds., 403-415.

Sgall, Petr. 1960. Obixodno-razgovornyj češskij jazyk. *Voprosy jazykoznanija*, no. 2:11-20.

———. 1962. Znovu o obecné češtině. *Slovo a slovesnost* 23 (1):37-45.

———. 1963. K diskusi o spisovné a obecné češtině. *Slovo a slovesnost* 24 (4):244-254.

———. 1994. Sociological Issues of Spoken Language. In Čmejrková et al., eds., 137-144.

———. 1998a. Neochozujme spisovnou češtinu. *Český jazyk a literatura* 49 (1-2):29-35.

———. 1998b. Problems of Dialogue Research in Spoken Czech. In Čmejrková et al., eds., 502-506.

———. 1999. Čekající možnosti a číhající propasti. *Slovo a slovesnost* 60:161-175.

Sgall, Petr and Jiří Hronek. 1992. *Čeština bez příkras*. Prague: Nakladatelství H&H.

———. 1993. Speakers' Attitudes Towards Code Switching. In Eckert, ed., 50-62.

Sgall, Petr, et al. 1992. *Variation in Language*. Amsterdam & Philadelphia: John Benjamins.

Short, David. 1991. Living Czech: The Language of the He(a)rd. *Slavonic and East European Review* 69:502-510.

———. 1992. Common Czech and Common Literature: The Case of Frýbort. *Slavonic and East European Review* 70:201-212.

Singh, Udaya Narayana. 1986. Diglossia in Bangladesh and Language Planning Problems. In Fishman, et al., eds., 431-449.

*Slovník spisovného jazyka českého*. 1960-1971 (1989). Prague: Academia.

SSJČ – See entry under *Slovník spisovného jazyka českého*.

Starý, Zdeněk. 1993. The Forbidden Fruit is the Most Tempting, or Why There is no Czech Sociolinguistics. In Eckert, ed., 79-95.

Stich, Alexandr. 1987. On the Beginnings of Modern Standard Czech. In *Explizite Beschreibung der Sprache und automatische Textbearbeitung* 14:121-128. Prague: Matematicko-fyzikální fakulta Univerzity Karlovy.

———. 1995. Česká spisovnost a nespisovnost: kořeny a přítomnost. In Jančáková et al., eds., 49-55.

Širokova, A. G. 1955. Iz istorii razvitija literaturnogo češskogo jazyka. *Voprosy jazykoznanija*, no. 4:35-54.

Šrámek, R., ed. 1996. *Spisovnost a nespisovnost dnes*. Brno: Masarykova univerzita.

Štícha, František. 1996. Spisovnost a nespisovnost literární řeči vypravěče. In Šrámek, ed., 188-190.

Těšitelová, Marie et al. 1987. *O češtině v číslech*. Prague: Academia.

Thomas, George. 1991. *Linguistic Purism*. London: Longman.

————. 1996a. The Prague School Theory of Language Cultivation or Purism by the Backdoor. *Canadian Slavonic Papers* 38, no. 1-2:195-204.

————. 1996b. Towards a History of Modern Czech Purism: The Problem of Covert Germanisms. *Slavonic and East European Review* 74:401-420.

Tobin, Yishai. 1994. A Unified Analysis of Contractions in English in Spoken and Written Discourse. In Čmejrková et al., eds., 153-166.

Townsend, Charles. 1990. *A Grammar of Spoken Prague Czech*. Columbus OH: Slavica.

————. 1993. Colloquial Czech in Two Works of Literature: Landovský and Svoboda. In Eckert, ed., 96-110.

Trost, Pavel. 1987. Code Switching. In *Explizite Beschreibung der Sprache und automatische Textbearbeitung* 14:151-156. Prague: Matematicko-fyzikální fakulta Univerzity Karlovy.

ÚJČ — See entry under Ústav pro jazyk český.

Uličný, Oldřich. 1995. K teorii mluveného jazyka. In Jančáková et al., eds., 19-25.

————. 1998. K článku prof. Sgalla „Neochozujme spisovnou češtinu". *Český jazyk a literatura* 49 (1-2):35-39.

Ústav pro jazyk český (ÚJČ), eds. 1979. *Aktuální otázky jazykové kultury v socialistické společnosti*. Prague: Academia.

Vachek, Josef. 1989. *Written Language Revisited*. Amsterdam and Philadelphia: John Benjamins.

Wald, Paul. 1986. Diglossia Applied: Vernacular Mixing and Functional Switching with Bangui Yakomas. In Fishman, et al., eds., 417-430.

## Appendices

### Appendix 1. The Czech alphabet and IPA phonemic equivalents

| letter | IPA | notes | letter | IPA | notes |
|--------|-----|-------|--------|-----|-------|
| a | a | | ň | ɲ | |
| á | aː | | o | o | |
| b | b | | ó | oː | |
| c | t͡s | | p | p | |
| č | t͡ʃ | | q | k | foreign words only |
| d | d | | r | r | |
| ď | j | | ř | r̝ | palatal trill/flap |
| e | ɛ | | s | s | |
| é | ɛː | | š | ʃ | |
| ě | jɛ | see 1 | t | t | |
| f | f | | ť | c | |
| g | g | | u | u | |
| h | ɦ | | ú | uː | as ů |
| ch | x | treated as single letter | ů | uː | as ú |
| i | ɪ | as y; see 2 | v | v | |
| í | iː | as ý; see 2 | w | v | foreign words only |
| j | j | | x | ks | foreign words only |
| k | k | | y | ɪ | as i; see 2 |
| l | l | | ý | iː | as í; see 2 |
| m | m | | z | z | |
| n | n | | ž | ʒ | |

1. The letter *ě* is pronounced [jɛ] after *p, b, f, v*. After *t, d, n, m* it gives the clusters the values [cɛ], [jɛ], [ɲɛ], [mɲɛ].

2. Consonantal letters followed by *y, ý, i, í* have the values indicated in the chart, except that *t, d, n* followed by *i, í* are pronounced [cɪ], [jɪ], [ɲɪ], [ciː], [jiː], [ɲiː].

3. The major ways in which standard pronunciation deviates from the pronunciation indicated in the table are: devoicing of *b, d, ď, g, h, ř, v, z, ž* in word-final position; regressive voicing assimilation in consonant clusters affecting *b, d, ď, f, g, h, ch, k, p, ř, s, š, t, ť, v, z, ž*; addition of a glottal hiatus before most word-initial and root-initial vowels.

IPA equivalents are taken from Dankovičová 1999:70-73.

## Appendix 2. Glossary of morphology chart abbreviations

The items are listed by CC variant. SC variants are given at the end of each entry.

1. *bysem* – first-person singular. conditional auxiliary (SC *bych* 'I would')
2. *bysme* – first-person plural conditional auxiliary (SC *bychom* 'we would')
3. *dobrý auta* – levelled neuter nominative plural adjective form (SC *dobrá auta* 'good cars')
4. *dobrý hráči* – levelled masculine animate nominative plural adjective form (SC *dobří hráči* 'good players')
5. *dělaj/sázej* – truncation of third-person plural non-past form (SC *dělají/sázejí* 'they do/they gamble')
6. *lidi* – levelling of irregular masculine animate nominative plurals (SC *lidé* 'people')
7. *můžou* – elimination of velar–palatal alternation in the third-person plural non-past of consonantal stem verbs (SC *mohou* 'they can')
8. *můžu* – elimination of velar–palatal alternation in the first-person singular non-past of consonantal stem verbs (SC *mohu* 'I can')
9. *nes* – truncated past participle of consonantal stem verbs (SC *nesl* 'he carried')
10. *pánama/kostma* – instrumental plural form in *-ma* (SC *pány/kostmi* 'men/bones')
11. *pracujou* – third-person plural non-past of "class 6" verbs following a palatal consonant (SC *pracují* 'they work')
12. *pracuju* – first-person singular non-past of "class 6" verbs following a palatal consonant (SC *pracuji* 'I work')
13. *prosej(í)* – levelling of third-person plural ending for "class 3 and 4" verbs to the "class 3 "ending (SC *prosí* 'they ask')
14. *říct* – levelling of *-ci* infinitives to more common *-t* pattern (SC *říci* 'to say')
15. *s dobrym* – shortening of masculine and neuter instrumental and locative singular adjectives (SC *s dobrým, o dobrém* 'with good, about good'; also CC *s dobrým, o dobrým*)
16. *sází* – levelling of third-person plural ending for "class 3 and 4" verbs to the "class 4" ending (SC *sázejí* 'they gamble')
17. *vedem* – use of shorter first-person plural non-past ending in "class 1, 2, 6" verbs (SC *vedeme* 'we lead')

## Appendix 3.  The four major phonological correspondences between SC and CC

| Alphanumeric label | Description | Conventional notation | | |
|---|---|---|---|---|
| **Type D:** | /ɛ:/ = /i:/ | SC *é* /ɛ:/ | = | CC *ý, í* /i:/ |
| **Subtype D1:** | desinence-final | SC *-é* /-ɛ:/ | = | CC *-ý, -í* /-i:/ |
| **Subtype D2:** | desinence-initial | SC *-éC* /-ɛ:C/ | = | CC *-ýC, -íC* /i:C/ |
| **Subtype D3:** | word roots | SC *-é-* /-ɛ:-/ | = | CC *-ý-, -í-* /-i:-/ |
| | | | | |
| **Type E:** | /i:/ = /ɛj/ | SC *ý* /i:/ | = | CC *ej* /ɛj/ |
| **Subtype E1:** | desinence-final | SC *-ý* /-i:/ | = | CC *-ej* /-ɛj/ |
| **Subtype E2:** | desinence-initial | SC *-ýC* /-i:C/ | = | CC *-ejC* /-ɛjC/ |
| **Subtype E3:** | word roots | SC *-ý-* /-i:-/ | = | CC *-ej-* /-ɛj-/ |
| | | | | |
| **Type F:** | /o/ = /vo/ | SC *o* /o/ | = | CC *vo* /vo/ |
| **Subtype F1:** | word-initial | SC *#o* /#o/ | = | CC *#vo* /#vo/ |
| **Subtype F2:** | root-initial, word-internal | SC *%o* /%o/ | = | CC *%vo* /%vo/ |
| | | | | |
| **Type G:** | /u:/ = /ou/ | SC *ú* /u:/ | = | CC *ou* /ou/ |
| **Subtype G1:** | word-initial | SC *#ú* /#u:/ | = | CC *#ou* /#ou/ |
| **Subtype G2:** | root-initial, word-internal | SC *%ú* /%u:/ | = | CC *%ou* /%ou/ |

## Appendix 4. Corpus coding tags

**11-29: phonology**
11. SC é vs. CC ý terminally
12. SC é vs. CC ý non-terminal, in desinence
13. SC é vs. CC ý root-internal
14. SC ý vs. CC ej terminally
15. SC ý vs. CC ej non-terminal, in desinence
16. SC ý vs. CC ej root-internal
17. SC o vs. CC vo word-initially
18. SC o vs CC vo root-initially
19. SC ú vs. CC ou
20. SC long vowel vs. CC short vowel
21. SC consonant cluster vs. CC simplified form
22. SC jsem, jméno vs. CC sem, meno
23. SC short vowel vs. CC long vowel
24. problematic places (i.e. -énko vs. -ínko)

**30-69: morphology**
30. SC -mi, -y/i vs. CC -ma (nouns)
31. SC -mi vs. CC -ma (adjectives)
32. SC dobří vojáci vs. CC dobrý vojáci
33. SC Američané, lidé vs. CC Američani, lidi
34. SC malá města vs. CC malý města
35. SC s dobrým vs. CC s dobrym
36. SC o vojácích vs. CC vo vojákách
37. SC pane Nováku vs. CC pane Novák
38. SC dvou, dvěma vs. CC dvouch, dvoum (etc.)
39. SC mi vs. CC mě
40. SC mé vs. CC mojí (oblique)
41. SC ji vs. CC jí
42. SC obsazen, obsazený vs. CC obsazený
43. SC déle, etc. vs. CC dýl
50. SC děkuji vs. CC děkuju
51. SC dekují vs. CC děkujou
52. SC píši vs. CC píšu
53. SC píší vs. CC píšou
54. SC mohu, mohou vs. CC můžu, můžou
55. SC neseme vs. CC nesem
56. SC dělají, umějí vs. CC dělaj, uměj
57. SC bydlí vs. CC bydlej(í)
58. SC moci vs. CC moct
59. SC vedl vs. CC ved
60. SC řízl vs. CC říznul
61. SC bychom vs. CC bysme

62. SC bych vs. CC bysem
63. SC města byla vs. CC města byly
64. SC dříve vs. CC dřívějc
65. SC vzít taxík vs. CC vzít taxíka

**70-89: syntax**
70. SC který vs. CC co
71. SC jenž vs. CC co
72. SC jestli, pokud vs. CC když
73. SC rukou vs. CC s rukou
74. SC matka je učitelkou vs. CC matka je učitelka
75. SC přišel vs. CC von přišel
76. SC není to tak strašné vs. CC vono to není tak strašný
77. SC viděl jsem vs. CC já viděl
78. SC bylo slyšet dechovku vs. CC byla slyšet dechovka
79. SC -li vs. CC jes(t)li
80. SC udělal jsem to vs. CC mám uděláno
81. SC Viktorův vs. CC Viktora
82. SC ten muž tě nezná vs. CC to tě ten muž nezná

**90-99: lexicon**
90. knižní 'bookish' (within SC)
91. hovorové 'colloquial' (unclear; SC in a limited way, but also CC)
92. obecné 'common Czech' (within CC)
93. nízké 'low' (sometimes placed within CC)
94. vyšší slang 'higher slang' (sometimes placed within CC)
95. nižší slang 'lower slang' (sometimes placed within CC)
96. SC jsi vs. CC (j)seš (CC)
97. běžné 'ordinary' (CC terms gaining currency, acc. to Sgall and Hronek 1992)
98. problematic words (not listed in sources; obvious errors; sources disagree)

## Appendix 5. Token counts

### Phonology: token counts

| no. | description | Pr - CC | Pr - SC | Ko - CC | Ko - SC | Kl - CC | Kl - SC |
|-----|-------------|---------|---------|---------|---------|---------|---------|
| D1 | *velký auto*<br>-iː = -ɛː | 139/188 =<br>73.9% | 49/188 =<br>26.1% | 44/120 =<br>36.7% | 76/120 =<br>63.3% | 9/147 =<br>6.1% | 138/147 =<br>93.9% |
| D2 | *velkýho*<br>-iːC = ɛːC | 31/36 =<br>86.1% | 5/36 =<br>13.9% | 24/66 =<br>36.4% | 42/66 =<br>63.6% | 3/65 =<br>4.6% | 62/65 =<br>95.4% |
| D3 | *mlíko*<br>-iː- = -ɛː- | 7/12 =<br>58.3% | 5/12 =<br>41.7% | 5/13 =<br>38.5% | 8/13 =<br>61.5% | 2/17 =<br>11.8% | 15/17 =<br>88.2% |
| E1 | *velkej*<br>-ɛj = -iː | 59/87 =<br>67.8% | 28/87 =<br>32.2% | 39/97 =<br>40.2% | 58/97 =<br>59.8% | 0/101 =<br>0.0% | 101/101 =<br>100.0% |
| E2 | *velkejch*<br>-ɛjC = -iːC | 13/19 =<br>68.4% | 6/19 =<br>31.6% | 2/32 =<br>6.3% | 30/32 =<br>93.7% | 0/41 =<br>0.0% | 41/41 =<br>100.0% |
| E3 | *mlejn*<br>-ɛj- = -iː- | 33/72 =<br>45.8% | 39/72 =<br>54.2% | 15/57 =<br>26.3% | 42/57 =<br>73.7% | 2/66 =<br>3.0% | 63/66 =<br>97.0% |
| F1 | *vodejdu*<br>#vo = #o | 0/185 =<br>0.0% | 185/185<br>= 100.0% | 38/280 =<br>13.6% | 242/280 =<br>86.4% | 0/289 =<br>0.0% | 289/289 =<br>100.0% |
| F2 | *zavostalej*<br>%vo = %o | 0/3 =<br>0.0% | 3/3 =<br>100.0% | 1/6 =<br>16.7% | 5/6 =<br>83.3% | 0/7 =<br>0.0% | 7/7 =<br>100.0% |
| G | *ouřad*<br>ou = uː | 1/19 =<br>5.3% | 18/19 =<br>94.7% | 0/19 =<br>0.0% | 19/19 =<br>100.0% | 0/16 =<br>0.0% | 16/16 =<br>100.0% |

*Notes:*

All features listed in appendix 4 were coded and retrieved, but of the morphological and phonemic features only those listed here were found in significant enough numbers.

Syntactic and lexical features are by and large not listed here, as token counts were given in chapter 5. The only syntactic and/or lexical features given below are those that can be interpreted as morphological (e.g. facultative animates, gender of plural verb participles)..

**Morphology token counts**

| no. | description | Pr - CC | Pr - SC | Ko - CC | Ko - SC | Kl - CC | Kl - SC |
|-----|-------------|---------|---------|---------|---------|---------|---------|
| 10 | *knih<u>ama</u>*<br>*-ma = -mi* | 3/6 =<br>50% | 3/6 =<br>50% | 1/5 =<br>20% | 4/5 =<br>80% | 3/6 =<br>50% | 3/6 =<br>50% |
| 10 | *muž<u>ema</u>,*<br>*slov<u>ama</u>*<br>*-ma = y/i* | 2/6 =<br>33.3% | 4/6 =<br>66.7% | 5/12 =<br>41.7% | 7/12 =<br>58.3% | 2/10 =<br>20% | 8/10 =<br>80% |
| 10 | *s váma*<br>*-ma = -mi* | 6/6 =<br>100.0% | 0/6 =<br>0.0% | 5/8 =<br>62.5% | 3/8 =<br>37.5% | 3/9 =<br>33.3% | 6/9 =<br>66.7% |
| 10 | *total these*<br>*three rows* | 11/18 =<br>61.1% | 7/18 =<br>38.9% | 11/25=<br>44.0% | 14/25 =<br>56.0% | 8/25 =<br>32.0% | 17/25 =<br>68.0% |
| 10 | *mil<u>ejma</u>*<br>*-ejma = ými* | 3/6 =<br>50.0% | 3/6 =<br>50.0% | 1/3 =<br>33.3% | 2/3 =<br>66.7% | 1/7 =<br>14.3% | 6/7 =<br>85.7% |
| 4 | *dobrý hráči*<br>*ý = í* | 1/3 =<br>33.3% | 2/3 =<br>66.7% | 6/10 =<br>60.0% | 4/10 =<br>40.0% | 0/19 =<br>0.0% | 19/19 =<br>100.0% |
| 6 | *lid<u>i</u>*<br>*i = ové, é* | 3/3 =<br>100.0% | 0/3 =<br>0.0% | 4/4 =<br>100.0% | 0/4 =<br>0.0% | 17/22 =<br>77.3% | 5/22 =<br>22.7% |
| 3 | *dobrý auta*<br>*ý = á* | 3/3 =<br>100.0% | 0/3 =<br>0.0% | 2/3 =<br>66.7% | 1/3 =<br>33.3% | 2/14 =<br>14.3% | 12/14 =<br>85.7% |
| 15 | *s dobrym*<br>*ym = ým* | 0/9 =<br>0.0% | 9/9 =<br>100.0% | 1/10 =<br>10.0% | 9/10 =<br>90.0% | 0/4 =<br>0.0% | 4/4 =<br>100.0% |
| -- | *vo voják<u>ách</u>* | --- | --- | --- | --- | 0/1 = 0.0% | 1/1 =<br>100.0% |
| -- | *pane Novák!*<br>*nom. < voc.* | 1/1 =<br>100.0% | 0/1 =<br>0.0% | 1/4 =<br>25.0% | 3/4 =<br>75.0% | 0/5 =<br>0.0% | 5/5 =<br>100.0% |
| -- | *dative*<br>*mě/mně =*<br>*mi* | 0/78 =<br>0.0% | 78/78 =<br>100.0% | 6/77 =<br>7.8%<br>(3 mě, 3<br>mně) | 71/77 =<br>92.2% | 0/55 =<br>0.0% | 55/55 =<br>100.0% |

## Morphology token counts, continued

| no. | description | Pr - CC | Pr - SC | Ko - CC | Ko - SC | Kl - CC | Kl - SC |
|-----|-------------|---------|---------|---------|---------|---------|---------|
| -- | *mojí, -ích,*<br>*-ím = mé,*<br>*mých, mým* | 2/11 =<br>18.2% | 9/11 =<br>81.8% | 0/42 =<br>0.0% | 42/42 =<br>100.0% | 0/12 =<br>0.0% | 12/12 =<br>100.0% |
| -- | *obsazený*<br>*= obsazen* | --- | --- | 12/28 =<br>42.9%<br>(3m, 7f,<br>2pl) | 16/28 =<br>57.1%<br>(9m, 3f,<br>2pl, 2n) | 13/16 =<br>81.3%<br>(3m, 2f,<br>3n, 5mp) | 3/16 =<br>18.7%<br>(2f, 1pl) |
| -- | *dýl, víc*<br>*= déle, více* | 34/34 =<br>100.0% | 0/34 =<br>0.0% | 45/46 =<br>97.8% | 1/46 =<br>2.2% | 27/27 =<br>100.0% | 0/27 =<br>0.0% |
| -- | *mít vzteka*<br>*(facultative*<br>*animacy)* | vředa,<br>pokra,<br>búra (2),<br>taxíka,<br>chleba | --- | vzteka (2) | --- | taxíka (2) | --- |
| -- | *moje, moji*<br>*= mé, má,*<br>*mí, mou* | 9/14 =<br>64.3% | 5/14 =<br>35.7% | 10/29 =<br>34.5% | 19/29 =<br>65.5% | 13/15 =<br>86.7% | 2/15 =<br>13.3% |
| 12 | *pracuju*<br>*ju = ji* | 25/25 =<br>100.0% | 0/25 =<br>0.0% | 26/28 =<br>92.9% | 2/28 =<br>7.1% | 20/20 =<br>100.0% | 0/20 =<br>0.0% |
| 11 | *pracujou*<br>*jou = jí* | 2/5 =<br>40.0% | 3/5 =<br>60.0% | 3/4 =<br>75.0% | 1/4 =<br>25.0% | 7/25 =<br>28.0% | 18/25 =<br>72.0% |
| 12 | *píšu*<br>*Ču = Či* | 5/5 =<br>100.0% | 0/5 =<br>0.0% | --- | --- | 4/4 =<br>100.0% | 0/4 =<br>0.0% |
| 11 | *píšou*<br>*Čou = Čí* | --- | --- | --- | --- | 3/3 =<br>100.0% | 0/3 =<br>0.0% |
| 12 | *total all 12* | 30/30 =<br>100.0% | 0/30 =<br>0.0% | 26/28 =<br>92.9% | 2/28 =<br>7.1% | 24/24 =<br>100.0% | 0/24 =<br>0.0% |
| 11 | *total all 11* | 2/5 =<br>40.0% | 3/5 =<br>60.0% | 3/4 =<br>75.0% | 1/4 =<br>25.0% | 10/24 =<br>41.7% | 14/24 =<br>58.3% |

## Morphology token count, continued

| no. | description | Pr - CC | Pr - SC | Ko - CC | Ko - SC | Kl - CC | Kl - SC |
|-----|-------------|---------|---------|---------|---------|---------|---------|
| 8 | *můžu* *Ču < Ku* | 20/20 = 100.0% | 0/20 = 0.0% | 7/12 = 58.3% | 5/12 = 41.7% | 19/19 = 100.0% | 0/19 = 0.0% |
| 7 | *můžou* *Čou < Kou* | 3/3 = 100.0% | 0/3 = 0.0% | 2/2 = 100.0% | 0/2 = 0.0% | 4/4 = 100.0% | 0/4 = 0.0% |
| -- | *total all 7 & 8* | 22/22 = 100.0% | 0/22 = 0.0% | 9/14 = 64.3% | 5/14 = 35.7% | 23/23 = 100.0% | 0/23 = 0.0% |
| 17 | *vedem* *-em = -eme* | 45/57 = 78.9% | 12/57 = 21.1% | 16/18 = 88.9% | 2/18 = 11.1% | 0/31 = 0.0% | 31/31 = 100.0% |
| 5 | *dělaj* *aj = ají* | 6/13 = 46.2% | 7/13 = 53.8% | 0/15 = 0.0% | 15/15 = 100.0% | 0/51 = 0.0% | 51/51 = 100.0% |
| 5 | *sázej* *ej = ejí* | 6/7 = 85.7% | 1/7 = 14.3% | 1/4 = 25.0% | 3/4 = 75.0% | 0/14 = 0.0% | 14/14 = 100.0% |
| 13 | *prosej(í)* *ej(í) = í* | 5/7 = 71.4% | 2/7 = 28.6% | 4/15 = 26.7% | 11/15 = 73.3% | 0/57 = 0.0% | 57/57 = 100.0% |
| 14 | *říct* *ct = ci* | 12/12 = 100.0% | 0/12 = 0.0% | 11/11 = 100.0% | 0/11 = 0.0% | 7/7 = 100.0% | 0/7 = 0.0% |
| 9 | *nes* *-ø = -l* | 10/30 = 33.3% | 20/30 = 66.7% | 23/59 = 39.0% | 36/59 = 61.0% | 6/29 = 20.7% | 23/29 = 79.3% |
| 2 | *-bysme* *-sme = -chom* | 0/13 = 0.0% | 13/13 = 100.0% | 0/3 = 0.0% | 3/3 = 100.0% | 0/14 = 0.0% | 14/14 = 100.0% |
| 1 | *-bysem* *-sem = -ch* | 0/49 = 0.0% | 49/49 = 100.0% | 1/33 = 3.0% | 32/33 = 97.0% | 0/39 = 0.0% | 39/39 = 100.0% |
| -- | *města byly* *-y = -a* | --- | --- | --- | --- | 0/1 = 0.0% | 1/1 = 100.0% |

# Name and subject index

This index contains personal names, proper names and concepts mentioned in the text and charts of the monograph. It does not contain entries for words like *morphology, hierarchy* or others which are found on every second or third page. The appendices are not indexed.

Alsatian 16
anacoluthon 68, 70, 72
analogy 3 2, 45, 55, 58, 61, 85, 88
animate subgender 18, 22, 23, 25, 36, 81, 88, 102
Arabic 9, 16, 114
aspect 22
Auer 95
Auty 12
Bednářová 35-37, 40, 50, 53-54, 56, 59, 60, 90 91, 100, 114
Biber 6, 7, 68
bilingualism 7, 9, 17, 98, 113, 115
Bílý 33, 43, 109
Bělič 13
Carpathian 17
Čermák 42, 42, 104, 108-109
Chloupek 14, 103, 108
Čmejrková 6
Cochran 10, 16
code alternation 9, 14, 34, 98
code mixing 5, 9, 14, 33, 34, 38, 46, 85, 96-99, 110, 111, 114
code-switching 5, 7-9, 15, 33, 34, 37, 38, 46, 65, 90, 94-99, 110-112
Colloquial Czech 13, 15, 45-47, 56, 73-78, 82, 84, 104-105, 109-110
communicative code-switching 8, 9, 33, 94, 95
contractions 6, 7
Cummins 90
Czech Language Institute 6, 12, 13, 31, 34
Daltas 115
Daneš 40, 45
Dankovičová 10, 21 ,122
Davidová 15, 45-46
De Silva 33
Dickins 12, 17, 33

diglossia 9, 10, 16, 33-34, 112, 113-115
discourse analysis 5
dislocation 68-69, 72
Ebonics 7-8
Eckert 7
ellipsis 61-62, 66-67, 68, 70-71, 72, 82, 84, 105
Ferguson 9-12, 18, 33, 34, 113, 114
Fishman 10, 33, 115
French 10, 16, 114
functional sentence perspective 68
Gair 33
Gammelgaard 1, 12, 13, 19, 23, 27, 29, 33-35, 47, 50, 54, 56, 59-61, 63, 65, 66, 68, 70, 73, 90, 91, 100, 106, 110, 114
Gardner-Chloros 16, 97-99
German 10, 12, 16, 114
Gotteri 1
Greek 10, 16
Grygar-Rechziegel 33
Guarani 10
Gumperz 34
Håkon 16
Hammer 33-35, 45, 50, 56, 65, 110, 111, 114
Havránek 13, 15, 20, 45, 46, 113
Hlavsová 16-17
Hoffmannová 6, 9
Hronek 14, 30, 41-42, 75-78, 82, 84, 100, 102, 104, 110, 111
Hudson, Richard 8, 34
Hungarian 17
hypotaxis 6, 67-68
instrumentality 20, 62-64
interdialect 5, 14-15, 46
interruption 68, 71-72
intertextuality 33

Janda 8
Janicki 16
Kraus 34, 40, 54-55, 73
Kravčišinová 35-37, 40, 50, 53-54, 56, 59,
    60, 90 91, 100, 114
language culture 3, 31
language planning 3, 16
Micklesen 33
Milroy and Milroy 7
mood 22
Moravia 14-16, 42, 45, 46, 114
Müllerová 6, 9, 34, 37
National Revival 12
Nebeská 13
Norwegian 16
Paolillo 16, 33
paradigm 22-25
parataxis 6, 67-68
Polish 14, 113
portmanteau morph 22, 38
Prague school functionalism 12, 13
purism 3, 12, 13, 31, 45
relative pronouns 20, 62, 64-65, 82, 96,
    98, 105
repair 68-69, 72
repetition 68-69, 72
Romany 16, 17
Russian 8, 10, 113
Scotton 94, 98, 99
sentence length 65-66
sentence structure 65-68
Sgall 1, 9, 12-14, 17, 19, 27, 32, 33, 41,
    45, 46, 50, 65, 75-78, 82, 84, 102, 104,
    106, 109-112
Short 34, 47, 114
Silesia 15-16, 45-46, 114
Sinhala 16
situational code-switching 8, 9, 33, 94,
    115
Slovak 15, 16-17, 48
Spanish 8, 10
Starý 13
Stich 12
Swahili 16
Swartz 6
syncretism 22

Těšitelová 65-68
Thomas 12, 13, 45
Timberlake 8
Tobin 7
Townsend 12, 17, 21, 34, 35, 40, 45, 47,
    55, 63, 76, 103, 104
truncation 6, 45, 55, 56, 60, 61, 83, 87, 88
underground literature 47, 65, 68, 106
unfinished utterances 68, 71, 72
Vachek 5
Vietnamese 17
Yugoslavia 17

# Introduzione alla linguistica greca

## Moreno Morani
*Università degli Studi di Genova*

L'*Introduzione alla linguistica* greca intende offrire una breve guida per lo studio della lingua greca in una prospettiva di linguistica storica. La lingua greca presenta due singolari caratteristiche: la durata della sua attestazione (tre millenni e mezzo di storia) e la presenza di numerose varietà dialettali. Tenendo conto di questa premessa, il volume fornisce una panoramica generale delle problematiche fonda-mentali attinenti alla formazione e allo sviluppo storico della lingua, a partire dalla documentazione micenea: la lingua greca è esaminata nel quadro della famiglia linguistica indeuropea, e vengono analizzati, alla luce delle principali teorie proposte dagli studiosi, i rapporti tra la lingua greca e l'indeuropeo ricostruito, le relazioni con le altre lingue indeuropee, la presenza di elementi non indeuropei nel greco. Per il secondo aspetto, si presentano le principali questioni relative alla classificazione dei dialetti greci, dei quali si fornisce anche una sommaria descrizione.

Per quanto l'interesse fondamentale della trattazione riguardi il greco antico nelle sue principali manifestazioni letterarie, lo sviluppo della lingua è seguito dalla documentazione micenea fino al periodo bizantino e moderno. Il manuale è destinato agli studenti universitari e agli insegnanti di lingue e letterature classiche, e contiene quelle nozioni fondamentali di grammatica comparata e di storia della lingua che lo possano rendere utile per un primo orientamento in problematiche complesse che formano oggetto di discussioni complesse e talvolta secolari.

**Indice:**

PREMESSA - ABBREVIAZIONI
CAPITOLO PRIMO: Il greco e le lingue indeuropee
I. Le lingue indeuropee. II. Metodo, obiettivi e limiti della ricostruzione. III. Cenni di fonetica indeuropea. IV. Dall'indeuropeo al greco.

CAPITOLO SECONDO : I dialetti greci e il miceneo
I. I dialetti greci. II. Il miceneo.

CAPITOLO TERZO: La formazione del greco
I. Teorie a confronto. II. Greco e altre lingue indeuropee. III. Elementi non indeuropei nel greco.

CAPITOLO QUARTO: Lineamenti di cronologia del greco
I. Omero. II. La lingua della lirica. III. Il dramma attico. IV. La lingua della prosa. V. La koiné. VI. Verso il greco moderno.

Bibliografia, Indice

ISBN 3 89586 949 X.
**LINCOM Studies in Indo-European Linguistics 09.**
Ca. 260 pp. EUR 61.36 / DM 120 / USD 65 / £ 40.

# An Introduction to the Study of Morphology
VIT BUBENIK
*Memorial University of Newfoundland*

Each chapter (with the exception of the last one) is provided with pertinent exercises. Its data are taken from languags the author has been researching over the last twenty years (Latin, Greek, Turkish, Arabic, Hebrew, Sanskrit, Russian). Its argumentation is built around the major turning points in the history of morphology linked with scholars such as Hockett (1954), Matthews (1974), Bybee (1985), Dressler (1985), Bauer (1988), Spencer (1991), Carstairs-McCarthy (1992) and Aronoff (1993). In the last chapter the author explicates a cognitively conceived subdiscipline of Morphology in its relation to Formal Syntax, Generative Phonology, Functional Grammar, so-called Natural Morphology, Universal Grammar, and Typology.

**Contents**: Introduction, Grammatical Units, Paradigmatic and Syntagmatic Relations, Inflectional and Derivational Morphology, Inflectional Categories Associated with Nominal Elements, Inflectional Categories Associated with Verbal Elements, Morphosyntactic Properties and their Exponents, Morpheme and Allomorph, Derivational Morphology, Theoretical Models of Morphology, References.

ISBN 3 89586 570 2.
LINCOM Coursebooks in Linguistics 07.
Ca. 220 pp. USD 48 / DM 72 / £ 28.


# Structure and Interpretation in Natural Language
MARC AUTHIER & LISA REED
*The Pennsylvania State University*

The central objective of this book is to present an integrated theory of the syntax-semantics interface, one which combines the most recent advances in the generative framework with the basic tenets of model-theoretic semantics. The three opening chapters develop, in a step-by-step and highly accessible fashion, an approach to structure and meaning in these terms.

The remaining chapters show how this approach sheds light on three long-standing issues in formal grammar: the treatment of "syntactically-triggered" presuppositions, the treatment of some notable exceptions to the generative binding conditions, and the issue of the relative autonomy of syntax and semantics. With respect to the first issue, it is argued that a compositional treatment of syntactically-triggered presuppositions can be formulated as a condition which ties presuppositional triggers to a specific class of syntactic configurations definable in terms of devices found in Minimalist syntax. A subsequent chapter demonstrates that the empirical coverage of so-called Bare-Output Conditions in generative syntax can be increased if such conditions are made sensitive to the two types of semantic information which have sometimes been recognized in model-theoretic semantics; that is, extension expressions and implicature expressions. Finally, empirical evidence is adduced which supports the view that there are two distinct types of semantic constraints and that those which make reference to features of tree geometry can, under specific circumstances defined by representational Economy conditions, override those which do not.

Audience: Linguists, philosophers, computational and psycho-linguists, cognitive scientists; advanced undergraduates, graduate students and researchers in these fields.

ISBN 3 89586 603 2.
LINCOM Studies in Theoretical Linguistics 14.
210pp. USD 70 / DM 112 / £ 42.

# Introduction to Linguistic Field Methods

BERT VAUX & JUSTIN COOPER
*Harvard University*

The present volume addresses the need for an up-to-date, accessible, and comprehensive introduction to the elicitation of linguistic data from native speaker informants. The material, following an introductory chapter surveying the general enterprise of field research, is organized into eight major areas of current linguistic and anthropological interest: Phonetics, Phonology, Morphology, Syntax, Semantics, Sociolinguistics/ Dialectology, Lexicography, and Folklore. The chapters are designed to be covered at a rate of one per week, based on a sixteen-week semester. Each chapter presents basic structures to be elicited, and provides cautionary tales drawn from the experiences of seasoned field workers who have attempted to elicit these structures. These, in turn, are followed by suggested readings and illustrative exercises for each chapter. Emphasis is placed not on developing a theory of field work, but rather on providing enlightening suggestions and entertaining anecdotes designed to guide students down their own personal path to linguistic discovery.

ISBN 3 89586 198 7.
LINCOM Coursebooks in Linguistics 01.
Ca. 240 pp. USD 48 / DM 72 / £ 28.

# Coursebook in Feature Geometry

JOHN NEWMAN
*Massey University*

The *Coursebook in Feature Geometry* is an undergraduate course introducing students to current phonology through a sustained use of the Feature Geometry framework. It is written as a coherent, accessible, and well-illustrated introduction to the key ideas of Feature Geometry, focusing on rules of assimilation. In its 20 units and 40 exercises, it takes the reader step-by-step through the representational devices of Feature Geometry. The *Coursebook* attempts to present the core ideas of Feature Geometry in a unified way, rather than attempting to incorporate the (considerable) debate concerning almost every aspect of the theory. The version of Feature Geometry underlying the *Coursebook* is basically that found in Sagey's The *Representation of features in non-linear phonology* (1990), revised in accordance with the claims of Lahiri and Evans' 1991 article on *Palatalization and coronality*.

The author is Senior Lecturer in the Department of Linguistics and Second Language Teaching, *Massey University*, New Zealand. The author has a PhD in linguistics from the University of California at San Diego.

ISBN 3 89586 102 2.
LINCOM Coursebooks in Linguistics 02.
160pp. USD 39 / DM 64 / £ 25.